MW00965055

THE
COVERED BRIDGES
COOKBOOK

by
B. Carlson

 HEARTS & TUMMIES
Cookbook Co.
3544 Blakslee Street
Wever, IA 52658
800-571-2665

© 1995 B. Carlson

Reprinted 1997, 2000, 2006, 2009, 2011, 2012,
2014 & 2015

All rights reserved. No part of this book may be reproduced or transmitted in any form or by any means, electronic or mechanical, including photocopying, recording or by any informational storage or retrieval system, except by a reviewer who may quote brief passages in a review to be printed in a magazine or newspaper-without permission in writing from the publisher.

* * * * * * * * * *

Although the author has exhaustively researched all sources to ensure the accuracy and completeness of the information contained in this book, he assumes no responsibility for errors, inaccuracies, ommisions, or any inconsistency herein. Any slights of people or organizations are unintentional. Readers should consult an attorney or accountant for specific applications to their individual publishing ventures.

HEARTS & TUMMIES
Cookbook Co.
3544 Blakslee Street
Wever, IA 52658
800-571-2665

3

PREFACE

It comes as no surprise that lovers delight in spending an idle hour strolling through and around those old covered bridges.

There is something about the cool and dark interior of a covered bridge that makes it pleasant refuge from a busy busy world.

Even when a vehicle thunders through such a bridge, giving rise to that old-fashioned rattle and clatter . . . it is soon gone, and only the silence remains.

Yes, there's something special about a covered bridge.

FOREWORD

This is a book of recipes; a cookbook. But, it's kind of a special cookbook. The recipes are those selected from among the best in some special corners of the rural midwest . . . from the lands of the covered bridges. B. Carlson brings us hundreds of recipes from folks who know the special feelings that those rattly old covered bridges can create.

Prof. Phil Hey
Briar Cliff College
Sioux City, Iowa

TABLE OF CONTENTS

Dedicated to -
Kitty Kimble Beauchenne

Kitty taught me, when I was a child, that the best part of a fish dinner was the fun you have catching the fish.

APPETIZERS & BEVERAGES

SHRIMP MOLD

2 env. Knox gelatin	1 small can tomato soup
1 small can shrimp	3 small pkg. cream cheese
¾ C. celery (chopped fine)	1 C. mayonnaise
¾ C. onion (chopped fine)	Salt and pepper to taste

Dissolve gelatin in ¼ C. water. Bring soup to a boil and add gelatin and cream cheese. Let cool. Add mayonnaise, celery, onions, shrimp and seasoning. Let it form about 5 minutes in a well-greased ring mold. Serve with crackers.

SNACK MIX

2 pkg. oyster crackers	¼ tsp. garlic powder
1 C. oil	1 pkg. Hidden Valley Ranch Mix
¼ tsp. dill weed	(Herb)
¼ tsp. lemon pepper (opt.)	

Mix all together and put in a jar or can be heated in 200° oven for 20 minutes. Stir a couple of times.

ANNIVERSARY PUNCH

1 can pineapple juice
2 cans frozen lemonade
2 cans (large) frozen orange juice
4 qts. ginger-ale

4 pkgs. lemon Kool-Aid
  plus 1 T. orange Kool-Aid
1 lb. sugar (2 C.)

Mix all ingredients except for the ginger-ale. Chill. Just before serving add the ginger-ale. Serves 50.

ORANGE JULIUS

½ of a 6-oz. can frozen orange
  juice concentrate
½ C. milk
½ C. water

½ tsp. vanilla
2 T. sugar
8-10 ice cubes
1 egg (if desired)

Blend in blender until slushy. Makes 2 large glasses.

TOMATO CHEESE LOG

1 can whole tomatoes (well drained)	½ C. chopped onion
1 pkg. (8-oz.) cream cheese (softened)	¼ tsp. salt
8-oz. grated cheddar cheese	1/8-¼ tsp. red cayenne pepper
½ C. butter or margarine (softened)	8-oz. chopped English walnuts

In large bowl combine tomato pulp, cheeses, margarine, onion, salt and pepper. Beat until smooth; spoon equal amounts onto 2 large pieces of waxed paper. Roll into log shapes. Place in freezer 1 hour or until firm. Remove paper and roll logs into the nuts on another piece of waxed paper. Wrap in foil and keep in refrigerator.

PUNCH

2 pkgs. Kool-Aid	1 (46-oz.) can pineapple juice
2 C. sugar	1 qt. bottle Sprite, Ginger-ale
3 qts. water	or 7-Up

Orange Kool-Aid works well for golden wedding anniversaries.

VEGGIE DIP

1 C. Hellman's mayonnaise
1 C. sour cream

1 T. dill seed
1 tsp. Beau Monde

Mix thoroughly and chill overnight.

COOL SUMMER SLUSH

2 bananas
1 (19-oz.) can crushed pineapple
  (put through blender)
2 cans (28-oz.) pineapple juice

2 lge. cans frozen orange juice
2 lge. cans frozen pink lemonade
1 C. sugar
8 C. water

Put the bananas and the pineapple through the blender. Add the pineapple juice, orange juice and lemonade. Boil the sugar and water and add the the first mixture. Freeze in large containers. To use fill glass ½ full of slush and add ginger-ale or 7-up to fill glass.

BLUE PUNCH

1 gal. cold water
½ C. sugar
11 small cans frozen lemonade
   (without water)

Scant T. blue food coloring
¼ tsp. green food coloring
11 (12-oz.) bottles 7-Up
½ gal. pineapple sherbet

Mix together in large container. Put in punch bowl; add scoops of sherbet and swish around so it melts and punch gets rather frothy. Serves approximately 135 3-oz. servings.

SPICED WALNUTS

1 qt. English walnuts
1 tsp. cinnamon
½ tsp. cloves

¼ tsp. allspice
1 C. sugar
3 T. water

Spread nuts in a single layer on a cookie sheet. Combine spices. Sprinkle ½ of mixture over nuts. Bake at 200° for 10 minutes. Combine sugar, water and remaining spices. Mix well. Bring to boil over medium heat. Continue cooking until a small amount dropped in cold water forms a soft ball. Pour syrup over warm nuts; mix quickly.

ROSETTES

1½ C. flour
2 tsp. sugar
¼ tsp. salt

1 C. milk
2 eggs

Sift dry ingredients. Combine milk and eggs in bowl and beat well. Add dry ingredients and beat until smooth and the consistency of thick cream. Heat fat to 360°-375°F. Heat iron in fat and dip into batter just even with top of iron (not over top). Dipping iron in fat before each rosette is made makes them easier to remove. Put in hot fat and cook until brown. When cool, sprinkle with powdered sugar or fill with favorite spread. Makes 48-50 shells.

Irons: If rosettes stick, the batter may be too thin so a small amount of flour should be added. Rosette or Patty Shell Irons may be purchased in the houseware department of large department stores.

RAW VEGETABLE DIP

2 C. sour cream
1 C. Kraft Real Mayonnaise
1 T. dill weed

1 T. minced onions
1 T. parsley flakes
Dash of seasoned salt

Combine sour cream, mayonnaise and seasonings; mix well and chill several hours. Serve with carrot sticks, celery sticks, raw cauliflower, pepper strips, etc. Makes 3 C.

OLIVE NUT SPREAD

6-oz. cream cheese
½ C. mayonnaise

½ C. chopped green olives
½ C. chopped pecans

Mix cheese and mayonnaise; add olives and nuts. Refrigerate overnight. Serve or cocktail bread.

LITTLE PIZZAS

1 lb. longhorn cheese
1 bunch green onions
1 small can chopped olives
¼ C. Wesson oil
1 can tomato sauce

2 T. catsup
1 T. Worcestershire sauce
1½ tsp. oregano
Dash Tobasco
1 pkg. English muffins

Combine all ingredients. Spread over muffins; broil until bubbly and slightly brown. Cut into bite-size pieces.

EASY CREAM CHEESE BALL

8-oz. cream cheese
¼ lb. butter or margarine

⅓ C. finely chopped nuts
1 small onion (minced) 2 T.

Soften cheese and butter and cream together with onion. Form into ball shape in bowl, cover with square of aluminum foil, and chill until firm. Chop nuts, place on same square of foil, and turn cheese ball out onto nuts. Roll around using foil to protect fingers, wrap securely, and chill again. Remove 30 minutes before serving with favorite cracker or vegetable relish.

EASY TACO MUNCHIES

1 lb. hamburger
1 bag taco chips

8-oz. taco sauce
4-oz. cheddar cheese (shredded)

Preheat oven to 300°. While it's heating, brown hamburger and drain well. Stir in ½ bottle taco sauce, let simmer 3-5 minutes, stirring occasionally. Place 2 doz. chips on large cookie sheet; put 1 tsp. of tightly packed meat on each shell. Sprinkle a pinch of cheese over meat on each shell. Heat 3-5 minutes or until cheese melts; serve warm. If using microwave, 30-45 sec. will do to melt the cheese.

CRAB MEAT DIP

2 C. flaked or canned crab meat
1 small C. cucumber (chopped)
1 tsp. onion (minced)

3 T. mayonnaise
1 T. lemon juice
Salt and pepper to taste

Mix ingredients together. Can also be used as a sandwich filling.

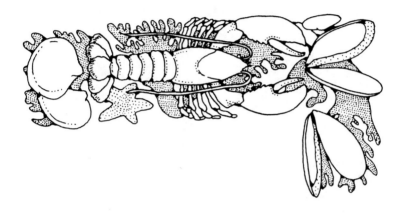

COCKTAIL MEATBALLS

2 lbs. ground beef
1 C. corn flake crumbs
⅓ C. parsley flakes
2 eggs
2 T. soy sauce

¼ tsp. pepper
½ tsp. garlic powder
⅓ C. catsup
2 T. minced onion
1 T. lemon juice

SAUCE:
1 (16-oz.) can cranberry sauce
1 (12-oz.) chili sauce

2 T. brown sugar

Combine beef, corn flakes, parsley, eggs, soy sauce, pepper, garlic, catsup and minced onion. Form mixture into small meatballs. Arrange meatballs in tray in the broiler. Broil until they are brown on both sides, 10 minutes. In a 2-qt. saucepan, combine cranberry sauce, chili sauce, brown sugar and lemon juice. Cook over moderate heat (250°), stirring occasionally until mixture is smooth and cranberry sauce is melted. Heat oven to 350°. In a 2-qt. pyrex bowl, arrange meatballs. Pour sauce over them and bake uncovered 30 minutes. Yield: 60 meatballs.

CRISP FRIED ONION RINGS

1 lge. Spanish or bermuda onion
½ C. flour
2 T. cornmeal

¾ tsp. baking powder
½ tsp. salt
⅔ C. milk

Cut onion in ¼'' slices to make rings. Soak in ice water for 20 minutes. Drain; pat dry. Mix remaining ingredients. Dip rings into batter and allow excess to drip. Fry in hot oil (375°) a few at a time; turn once until golden brown. Drain and sprinkle with salt if desired.

CHEESE BALL

1 small cream cheese (softened)
1 lb. Velveete cheese (softened)
2 buds minced garlic
1 C. pecans (finely ground)

Dash of salt
1 C. Baco chips or crushed bacon
Chili powder
Paprika

Mix together thoroughly cheeses, garlic, pecans, salt and bacon. Form into 2-3 compact balls; roll in mixture of chili and paprika. Wrap in plastic wrap and store in refrigerator. (NOTE: Can use bacon flavored cheese in place of the Baco chips and ¼ of the Velveeta.)

CHEESE BALL

2 pkgs. (8-oz. ea.) cream cheese
¼ C. real mayonnaise
½ C. olives (chopped)

½ C. onion (minced)
4-oz. cheddar cheese (shredded)

Whip together all ingredients; chill. Form into a ball and roll in chopped pecans.

SALADS, DRESSINGS, SOUP & SAUCES

CRANBERRY SALAD

4 C. cranberries
Juice from 1 can crushed pineapple
2 C. sugar
2 pkg. unflavored gelatin

1 C. nutmeats
1 C. tokay grapes
1 C. pineapple (crushed)

Cook cranberries in juice of 1 can crushed pineapple and enough water to make 3½ C. liquid. Cool; add sugar and unflavored gelatin that has been dissolved in 3 T. cold water. Let cool until almost cold. Then add nuts (I use English walnuts), crushed pineapple, and grapes cut in quarters and seeded. Mix well. Pour in large mold and refrigerate until set.

SPAGHETTI FRUIT SALAD

2 C. spaghetti (boiled & blanched)
4 eggs (beaten)
½ C. lemon juice
2 C. powdered sugar
Dash of salt

6 medium apples (diced)
1 large can pineapple (crushed or tidbits)
2 C. whipped cream
Bananas, nuts, oranges (optional)

Combine eggs, lemon juice, sugar and salt. Cook until thick; cool. Add fruit and spaghetti. Refrigerate 12-24 hours. Add whipped cream. Serves 30-40. Can be cut in half.

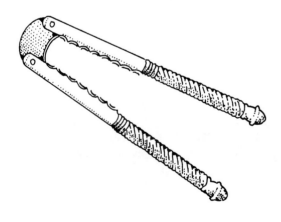

QUICK SPAGHETTI SAUCE

1 C. minced onion	½ C. oil
2 T. parsley flakes	1 tsp. salt
¼ tsp. pepper	1 tsp. Worcestershire sauce
8 drops Tabasco sauce	1 large bottle catsup

Saute onion. Add remaining ingredients. Cover and simmer ½ hour Add ½ - ¾ lbs.
of ground chuck (cooked). Simmer 10 minutes more.

SCANDINAVIAN SALAD

2 cans peas with onions	1 C. vinegar
1 can whole kernel corn	¼ C. oil
1 can French-cut beans	1½ C. sugar
1 jar pimentos	2 T. water
1 large, chopped onion	1 T. paprika
1 stalk celery (chopped)	

Drain well and mix together the peas with onions, whole kernel corn, French-cut
beans, pimentos, chopped onion and chopped celery. Mix together and pour over
the vegetables the vinegar, oil, sugar, water and paprika. Let stand 24 hours or
more in covered container. Keeps well up to 6 weeks in the refrigerator. The drained vegetable juice may be used for soups, stews, etc.

CELERY SEED OIL DRESSING

1 C. sugar
1 C. salad oil
½ C. vinegar
1 tsp. salt

1 tsp. dry mustard
1 T. celery seed
1 medium onion (quartered)

Store in covered jar in refrigerator.

CASSEROLE SAUCE MIX

2 C. instant non-fat dry milk crystals
¾ C. cornstarch
¼ C. instant chicken bouillon
2 T. dried onion flakes

1 tsp. dried thyme (crushed, opt.)
1 tsp. dried basil (crushed, opt.)
½ tsp. pepper

Combine all ingredients and store in airtight container. To use as substitute for 1 can condensed soup, mix ⅓ C. dry mix with 1 ¼ C. water in saucepan. Cook and stir until thickened. Add 1 T. margarine, if desired. (This is good for a fat-controlled and low-salt diet.)

SPICY CHILI

1 ½ lb. ground beef
½ C. chopped onion
1 (24-oz.) can tomato juice
1 (15½-oz.) can chili beans

2 T. Worcestershire sauce
1 (1.25-oz.) pkg. chili
  seasonings mix
1 tsp. ground cumin

Combine ground beef and onion in Dutch oven and cook until beef is browned, stirring to crumble meat; drain. Add remaining ingredients, mixing well. Cook over low heat 1 hour, stirring occasionally. Makes 8-10 servings.

MARINATED BROCCOLI

1 head cauliflower
2 stalks broccoli
1 large green pepper

1 stalk celery
Bacon (optional)

DRESSING:
1 C. sugar
1 T. salt
1 tsp. celery seed
1 C. vinegar

1 T. garlic salt
1 tsp. poppy seed
1 C. oil
1 tsp. paprika

Mix all dressing ingredients together and pour on vegetables. Refrigerate to marinate.

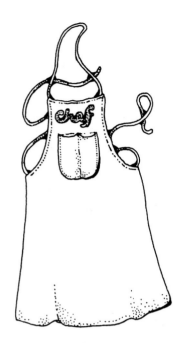

SPINACH SALAD

Layer in bowl:
1 bag spinach
1 can bean sprouts
2 hard-boiled eggs
1 can sliced water chestnuts

Fresh sliced mushrooms
Bacon crumbles
½ medium onion (chopped)

Well blended dressing:
½ C. oil
1/8 C. vinegar
⅓ C. sugar

¼ tsp. salt
1½ tsp. Worcestershire sauce

SPRING GARDEN SALAD

4 large ripe tomatoes (cut in chunks)
1 green pepper (cut in pieces)
1 cucumber (peeled and sliced)
1 onion (chopped or cut in rings)
2-3 stalks celery

Cauliflower (cut in pieces)
½ C. water
½ C. vinegar
½ C. sugar
½ C. oil

Mix all together and pour over vegetables. Salt to taste and let stand several hours. Drain some of liquid off before serving.

SHRIMP AND MACARONI SALAD

2 boxes small shell macaroni
2 (6½-oz.) cans cooked shrimp
1 C. diced celery

1 small onion (chopped)
1 C. diced green peppers

DRESSING:
½ C. catsup
½ C. oil
¼ C. vinegar

1 tsp. salt
⅔ C. sugar
Paprika (if desired)

Cook macaroni, drain. Mix all ingredients together and refrigerate for 24 hours.

WILTED LETTUCE

3-4 slices bacon
3-4 eggs
½ C. vinegar

½ C. water
1 C. sugar
Leaf or head lettuce

Brown bacon and chop, do not drain. Scramble eggs in grease and bacon. Mix vinegar, water and sugar and add to bacon and eggs. Let cool. Pour over lettuce and serve.

VEGETABLE SALAD

1 small head cauliflower (cut in pieces)
1 can sliced mushrooms
(drained and sliced)
1 small green pepper (chopped)

1 (3½-oz.) jar olives
¼ C. chopped onion
1 box chopped frozen broccoli

Mix all above ingredients. Just before serving put on one small bottle of Italian dressing.

VEGETABLE SALAD

1 small pkg. lemon or lime Jell-o
¾ tsp. salt
1 C. boiling water
¾ C. cold water
2 T. vinegar
2 T. grated onion

Dash of pepper
¾ C. finely chopped cabbage
¾ C. finely chopped celery
¼ C. finely chopped green pepper
2 T. diced pimento

Dissolve Jell-o and salt in boiling water; add cold water, vinegar, onion and pepper. Chill until very thick. Then fold in vegetables and pour into 1-qt. mold and chill until firm.

VEGETABLE SALAD

1 pkg. white gelatin
½ C. cold water
2 C. vinegar
½ C. sugar
1 tsp. salt

2 C. chopped cabbage
1 C. celery
Pimentos
1 pt. boiling water

Dissolve gelatin in hot water. Add rest of ingredients and chill.

CHICKEN SALAD

4-6 large chicken breasts
1 can pineapple chunks (drained)
1 can mandarin oranges (drained)

2 C. celery (sliced)
2 C. seedless grapes
1 pkg. toasted almonds (sliced)

DRESSING:
1 C. mayonnaise
1 C. sour cream
2 T. lemon juice

2 T. parsley
1 pkg. dry Lipton onion soup mix

Cook and chunk chicken. Add fruits, celery and almonds. Mix the dressing and add to chicken.

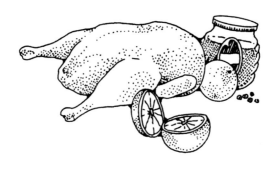

CAULIFLOWER SALAD

1 head cauliflower (broken into pieces)   1 C. nuts (chopped pecans
2 C. red seedless grapes (halved)   or peanuts)

DRESSING:
1 C. mayonnaise   2 tsp. mustard
½ C. sugar

Mix the salad ingredients together. Mix dressing ingredients. Add dressing to salad just before serving.

CARROT AND RAISIN SLAW

½ C. seedless raisins   1 T. vinegar
2 C. cabbage (shredded)   Mayonnaise
2 C. carrots (shredded)

Rinse raisins in hot water and drain. Combine rest of ingredients with enough mayonnaise to moisten the above ingredients. Garnish on lettuce.

FRESH CARROT MOLD

1 (3-oz.) pkg. lemon flavored Jell-o   1 C. grated carrots
1 C. boiling water   1 tsp. lemon juice
1 C. pineapple yogurt

Dissolve gelatin in boiling water and chill until slightly thickened. Fold in yogurt, carrots and lemon juice. Pour into mold and chill until firm. Unmold and serve on bed of lettuce with your favorite salad dressing.

EGG SALAD MOLD

14 hard-cooked eggs   ½ C. diced celery
1 qt. mayonnaise   ½ C. diced bell pepper
2 envelopes Knox gelatin   ½ C. diced onion greens
1 C. water   2 tsp. salt
½ C. sweet pickle relish   ¼ tsp. pepper

Dissolve gelatin in water. Mash or dice peeled eggs. Add mayonnaise, gelatin, salt and pepper. Mix well. Add remaining ingredients. Stir and pour into a greased angel cake pan or Jell-o mold. Refrigerate for 1 hour or more. Serves 15-20.

BOILED DRESSING (POTATO SALAD)

1 C. sugar
¾ tsp. salt
3 T. flour
3 eggs (beaten slightly)

¾ C. vinegar
½ C. water
1 T. butter

Mix dry ingredients and mix with beaten eggs. Add vinegar and water and mix thoroughly. Cook over low heat, stirring constantly until quite thick. Add butter.

CELERY SEED DRESSING

½ C. sugar
1 tsp. mustard
1 tsp. salt
1 tsp. onion (grated)

½ C. vinegar
1 C. salad oil
1 T. celery seed

Combine sugar, mustard, salt, onion and ½ of the vinegar; beat. Gradually add oil while beating, thick emulsion will form. Add remaining vinegar slowly. Add celery seed.

COOKED POTATO SALAD DRESSING

3 eggs
¾ C. sugar
½ C. white vinegar

1 C. Half and Half
1 tsp. salt

Beat the eggs, add the rest of the ingredients and beat. (I use rotary beater.) Cook until thickened over double boiler. Add a dash of pepper after cooked. Pour on cooled thin-sliced potatoes.

COLE SLAW DRESSING

1 C. sour cream
1 C. salad dressing
1 C. sugar

3 T. vinegar
1 tsp. celery seed
½ tsp. salt

Mix above ingredients. Makes 2-3 batches depending on amount of cabbage used.

BROCCOLI CHEESE SOUP

1 can cream of potato soup
(diluted with equal amounts of milk)
1 pkg. frozen chopped broccoli
(cooked and drained)

8-oz. processed cheese (Velveeta
makes it smooth, cheddar makes
a different texture)

Cook in crock pot and eat. Make a double recipe so there will be some left for the next day.

CHEESE SOUP

1 chicken bouillon cube
1½ C. potato (cubed)
1 C. water
½ C. celery (sliced)
½ C. carrot (sliced)
1½ C. cauliflower
¼ C. chopped onion

1 tsp. parsley flakes
½ tsp. salt
Pepper (dash)
1½ C. milk
2 T. flour
½ lb. Velveeta cheese

Cook all ingredients, except the milk, flour and cheese, together until the vegetables are tender. Add the rest and cook until done. You can also add broccoli if you like.

HAM CHOWDER

2-3 medium size potatoes	3 C. milk
3 T. chopped onion	1½ C. cooked ham (chopped)
3 T. margarine or butter	1½ C. shredded cheese
3 T. flour	Dash of pepper

Cook potatoes in boiling water; cube when cooled. Reserve liquid. Add enough water to make 1 C. in pan. In a soup kettle, saute onion in margarine until tender; not brown. Blend in flour and pepper. Add milk and potato water together. Cook until mixture thickens, stirring constantly. Add ham, potatoes and cheese. Stir until cheese melts. Serves 4-5 people. Can make ahead and keep hot in crock pot.

OLD FASHIONED CHICKEN SOUP

3 lb. chicken	1 stalk celery (diced)
1-2 tsp. salt	1 C. or more finely cut
1 diced onion	homemade noodles

Cover chicken with water and cook chicken until done. Remove chicken from bone and add the salt, onion and celery to stock. Then simmer until tender. Cut chicken into small pieces and return to soup (skim off fat). Add 1 C. finely cut homemade noodles. Simmer. Makes 6-8 servings.

CRANBERRY RELISH

(My sister shared this with us at Thanksgiving. I found it to be a very tasty way to serve your obligatory cranberries!)

4 C. whole fresh cranberries   1 whole orange (including peel)
1½ C. sugar (or less)   2 whole apples (including peel)

Grind berries and fruit together. Mix in sugar. Refrigerate 2-3 hours. Stir and serve. Can be refrigerated and kept for up to a week ahead.

CREAM OF ONION SOUP

¼ C. butter   ¼ tsp. salt
4 c. coarsely chopped onions   3 C. thin white sauce

WHITE SAUCE:
Cook until thickened:
3 T. butter or margarine   ¼ tsp. salt
1½ T. flour   Dash pepper
3 C. milk

Melt ¼ C. butter in microwave pan. Add chopped onions and salt. Cover and cook until onions are tender. Stir in the 3 C. white sauce and add 1 C. milk and heat thoroughly but don't boil. Serves 6.

HOT FUDGE SAUCE

4 sq. chocolate
½ C. margarine
½ tsp. salt

3 C. sugar
1 lge. can Pet evaporated milk

Heat chocolate and margarine in double boiler until melted. Add salt, sugar and milk. Stir occasionally until thickened. This recipe doesn't work if other brands of milk are used.

CHILI

2 lbs. ground beef
1 qt. water
2 medium sized onions
2 cans tomato sauce
5 whole allspice
½ tsp. red pepper
1 tsp. cumin seed
4 T. chili powder

½ sq. unsweetened chocolate
4 garlic cloves
2 T. vinegar
1 large bay leaf
5 whole cloves
2 tsp. Worcestershire sauce
1½ tsp. salt
1 tsp. cinnamon

In 4-qt. saucepan, add ground beef to water. Stir until beef separates into fine texture. Boil slowly for ½ hour. Add all other ingredients and bring to a boil and reduce heat and simmer uncovered for about 3 hours. Chili should be refrigerated overnight so fat can be skimmed from top before reheating. (Notice: No beans. It's a nice change.)

CLAM CHOWDER

2 slices bacon
½ C. onion
2 T. minced celery
2 (10-oz.) can minced clams
2½ C. diced potatoes
½ C. hot water
¼ C. dry white cooking wine

1 C. whipping cream
  or Half and Half
½ C. milk (I use more)
1 stick butter
1 tsp. salt
1/8 tsp. cayenne pepper
¼ tsp. white pepper

Cook potatoes until tender, but firm. Saute bacon, onions, celery, until translucent. Drain clams, but save liquid. Add the clam liquid, potato water and wine. Dice potatoes and add along with the rest of ingredients, except milk. Shortly before serving add milk and enough flour to thicken. Bring to boil and serve.

PIZZA SAUCE

2 qt. jars tomatoes (juice poured off)
1 large jar taco sauce (mild)
⅔ C. brown sugar
1 T. caraway seed
1 can tomato soup
1 tsp. oregano

1 tsp. sage
¼ tsp. pepper
2 shakes garlic powder
1 onion (chopped)
2 lbs. hamburger (cooked and
  drained)

Cook hamburger and drain. Mix all other ingredients together and cook down, 1½-2 hours, stirring occasionally. Enough sauce to make 4-5 pizzas. Freezes well.

SPAGHETTI SAUCE

1 lb. hamburger
1 medium onion
1 tsp. butter
1 can tomato sauce

1 can tomato soup
1 pt. tomatoes
3 T. brown sugar

Brown hamburger and onion. Add rest of ingredients. Cook slowly for 2 hours.

BASIC BARBECUE SAUCE

¼ C. salad oil
¾ C. chopped onion
1 C. honey
1 C. catsup
1 C. vinegar
½ C. Worcestershire sauce

1 T. dry mustard
1½ tsp. salt
1 tsp. oregano
1 tsp. pepper
½ tsp. thyme

Saute onions in hot oil. Add rest of ingredients; bring to boil. Turn heat down and cook 5 minutes. Scald 1 qt. fruit jar; cool. Cover and refrigerate. Excellent on meat.

CASSEROLES & VEGGIES

TWICE BAKED POTATOES

4 large baking potatoes   ½ tsp. salt
⅓ - ½ C. milk   Dash of pepper
¼ C. margarine   ¼ - ½ C. shredded cheddar cheese

Wash potatoes, scrubbing them well. Bake at 375° for 1 ¼ hours. Remove potatoes from the oven and increase oven temperature to 400°. Cut thin slice from top of each potato. Scoop out the inside, leaving a thin shell. Mash potatoes, adding milk, margarine and salt and pepper. Fill potato shells with the mashed potatoes and sprinkle with cheese. Bake 20 minutes or until golden brown.

RICE CASSEROLE

1 C. rice   ½ lb. grated longhorn cheese
½ C. celery   1 tsp. garlic salt
½ c. green pepper   ¼ C. Wesson oil
Small onion   ¾ C. milk

Cook 1 C. rice in 2 C. water. Add 1 tsp. salt; bring mixture to boil. Put lid on and let simmer 15 minutes. Let stand. Mix the celery, green pepper, onion and etc. with the rice and put in a greased 2-qt. casserole and bake 1 hour at 350°.

MACARONI AND CHEESE

1 C. elbow macaroni
  (cooked and drained)
⅔ of a 1-lb. box Velveeta cheese

¼ C. flour
1¼ C. milk

Cook macaroni in salted water until tender. Into a well greased 1½-qt. casserole put the cheese, torn into very small chunks. Add hot macaroni, flour and milk; stir and mix well. Bake at 325° for 15 minutes. Stir again and dash with pepper if desired. Return to oven and bake for another 30-35 minutes. Remove from oven and let set for 10 minutes before serving. Serves 4.

SPINACH CRUNCH

3 C. Rice Chex (crushed to 1½ C.)
1 tsp. onion powder
3 T. margarine (melted)
1 pkg. (8-oz.) cream cheese
1 can (5-oz.) evaporated milk
2 tsp. lemon juice
¾ tsp. seasoned salt

Dash of white pepper
1 (8-oz.) can sliced mushrooms
  (drained, reserve ⅓ C. liquid)
1 egg (well beaten)
1 pkg. (10-oz.) frozen chopped
  spinach (cooked and drained)

Combine chex and onion powder; stir in margarine; set aside. In pan, combine cream cheese, milk, lemon juice, seasonings and reserved mushroom liquid. Cook and stir over low heat until smooth. Add egg; cook, stirring constantly, until sauce thickens. Stir in mushrooms and spinach until well blended. Turn into shallow 1½-qt. casserole. Cover with crumbs. (Topping will be thick.) Bake at 350° for 15-20 minutes or until lightly browned and bubbly at edges. Makes 8 ½-C. servings.

STUFFING SIDE DISH

3 C. sage and onion bread crumbs
1 can cream of celery soup
½ can water
¼ C. celery

¼ C. onion
1 (4-oz.) can mushrooms (drained)
3 T. butter

Saute celery, onion, mushrooms in butter for 10-15 minutes; pour in soup and water. Heat until soup is warm. Place bread cubes in 2-qt. baking dish; pour soup mixture over bread cubes and mix. Bake for 25-30 minutes at 350°. Good with pork chops.

ONION PATTIES

¾ C. flour
2 tsp. baking powder
1 T. sugar
½ tsp. salt
1 T. corn meal

½ C. powdered milk
Cold water
2½ C. onions (finely chopped)
Fat for frying

Mix together first 6 ingredients; stir in enough cold water to make thick batter. Mix in onions and drop by teaspoonful into hot fat; flatten patties as you turn them. Fry to a golden brown. These are good and easier to make than onion rings.

GREEN RICE

1 large onion (chopped fine)	1 C. uncooked rice
2 stalks celery (chopped fine)	1 pkg. broccoli (cooked
1 can cream of celery soup	and chopped)
1 can cream of mushroom soup	1 small jar Cheez Whiz

Combine all ingredients in a large mixing bowl. Pour into a 2-qt. baking dish and bake at 350° for 45 minutes. Serve hot. Serves 6.

ELEGANT FRIED ONION RINGS

¼ C. oil	Dash garlic salt
½ C. flour	2 large or 3 medium onions
1 eg	1 C. flour
¾ C. milk	Oil for frying

In small bowl blend oil and flour with fork; add egg, then milk a little at a time. Stir in garlic salt and beat until smooth. Batter will be thin. Peel and slice onions; separate into rings. Put several rings in paper sack with 1 C. flour; shake gently to coat. Dip rings in batter. Remove one at a time into hot oil (375°); turn once. Take up when golden brown. Salt. Leftover onion rings can be reheated in a 425° oven for 2-3 minutes.

SWEET POTATO BAKE

4 sweet potatoes
½ C. brown sugar
1 T. cornstarch
¼ tsp. lemon juice
1 C. orange juice

¼ tsp. salt
¼ C. raisins
¼ C. butter
3 T. chopped walnuts (opt.)

Precook sweet potatoes until tender. Remove skins and cut potatoes in half, placing in baking dish. To make sauce, combine sugar, cornstarch and salt; then add orange juice, raisins and butter. Cook, stirring constantly, until thickened. Pour over potatoes in baking dish. If desired, sprinkle with walnuts. Bake in 350° oven for 20 minutes.

BAKED SLICED POTATOES

4 med. potatoes
¼ C. vegetable oil
1 tsp. salt

½ tsp. black pepper
½ tsp. thyme, oregano, sage
or basil

Preheat oven to 450°. Peel potatoes and cut into 1/8-inch slices. Place slices in bowl with oil, salt, pepper and herbs. Toss and mix well. Place slices in greased 15x10x1-inch bakin pan, overlapping slightly. Bake potatoes uncovered for 20 minutes, longer if you prefer them crisper.

CROCK POT POTATOES

1 small bag frozen hash browns
  (or grate your own in food processor)
1 can cream of potato soup

1 can cheddar cheese soup
Salt and pepper

Combine ingredients in crock pot and add milk to desired thickness. Cook on low setting 3-4 hours or until done.

CORN CASSEROLE

2 (12-oz.) cans white corn (drained)
  (yellow may be substituted)
½ C. chopped onion
¼ C. chopped bell pepper
1 C. cream of celery soup

1 (16-oz.) can French style green
  beans (drained)
½ C. chopped celery
¾ C. grated sharp cheese
1 (8-oz.) carton sour cream

TOPPING:
1 stick margarine

1 stack butter flavored crackers
  (Ritz type)

Mix all ingredients except those for topping. Place in 9x13-inch pan or casserole. Melt margarine and mix with crushed crackers. Spread evenly over vegetable mixture. Bake 350° for 45 minutes. Serves 12-15.

CABBAGE CASSEROLE

4 C. shredded cabbage
10¾-oz. can cream of
   potato soup
½ can water

1 C. grated
   cheddar cheese
Bread crumbs

Place the shredded cabbage in a greased quart baking dish and pour the soup mixed with water over it. Sprinkle cheese over the top and bake at 350° until the cabbage is tender. Remove from the oven and sprinkle with bread crumbs; return to oven to brown. Yields 6 servings.

RED CABBAGE

3 lbs. red cabbage
2-4 T. butter
2 T. sugar

1 T. vinegar
¾ C. red currant jelly

Remove outer leaves of cabbage and inner core and shred fine. Parboil with salt. Drain and add butter, sugar, vinegar and jelly. Cook gently until tender.

BROCCOLI AND CAULIFLOWER CASSEROLE

1 pkg. frozen broccoli
1 pkg. frozen cauliflower
1 can cream of celery soup

1 small jar Cheese Whiz
1 C. cooked Minute Rice

Cook broccoli and cauliflower as directed on package. Heat soup and cheese until melted together. Drain vegetables and mix with rice in a 9x13-inch pan. Pour cheese and soup over the top. Bake at 350° for 20 minutes.

DELICIOUS BROCCOLI CASSEROLE

30-oz. frozen broccoli
8-oz. Velveeta cheese (melted with
    ½ stick butter

1 tube of Ritz crackers (crushed
    with ½ stick butter (melted)

Place broccoli and cheese mixture in buttered casserole. Sprinkle with Ritz mixture. Cover with foil and bake for 20 minutes at 350°.

BARBECUE GREEN BEANS

3 cans green beans (drained)
1 onion, chopped
1 C. brown sugar

1 C. catsup
6 slices uncooked bacon
(cut in pieces)

Mix all ingredients and bake in covered casserole at 275° for 4 hours.

SCALLOPED CORN

¼ C. flour
1 can cream style corn
1 (3-oz.) cream cheese
½ tsp. onion salt
1 can whole kernel corn (drained)

1 can sliced mushrooms (drained)
½ C. shredded Swiss cheese
1½ C. soft bread crumbs
3 T. butter

Pour into pan. Bake at 400° for 10 minutes. On top put crumbs and butter and bake 10 minutes more.

HASH BROWN CASSEROLE

2 lb. bag frozen hash browns
  (Southern style)
1 medium onion (diced)
¼ C. butter (melted)
4-oz. grated sharp cheddar cheese

1 can sour cream
1 can cream of mushroom soup
Salt and pepper to taste
2 C. crushed corn flakes

Thaw potatoes. Toss with onion and butter. Blend cheese, sour cream, soup and salt and pepper mixture. Put in lightly greased 9x13-inch pan. Cover with crushed corn flakes tossed with melted butter. Cover with foil and bake at 350° for 25 minutes; remove foil and bake another 25 minutes or until done.

SWEET POTATO CASSEROLE

3 C. mashed sweet potatoes
  (2 cans 18-oz. vacuum packed)
1 C. white sugar
2 eggs
1 tsp. vanilla
½ C. butter or margarine

½ C. milk
½ C. brown sugar (packed)
½ C. flour
1 C. pecans or walnuts
½ C. butter

Mix the potatoes, sugar, eggs, vanilla, and butter and pour into buttered casserole. Mix the remaining ingredients and sprinkle on top. Bake at 350° for 45 minutes.

HARVARD BEETS

2 T. margarine
1 T. cornstarch
1 T. sugar

¼ tsp. salt
½ C. mild vinegar (white)
2 C. beets

Melt butter, add cornstarch, sugar and salt. Blend well, add vinegar slowly. Cook until thick. Add beets and heat thoroughly. Serves 4-6.

BROCCOLI AND MACARONI CASSEROLE

½ stick margarine
1 onion (diced)
2 pkgs. frozen broccoli (chopped)
1 C. Cheez Whiz

2 cans cream of mushroom soup
  (do not dilute)
2 C. big macaroni

Saute onion in margarine, add broccoli. Cook macaroni until tender. Put in buttered casserole dish in layers starting with macaroni then soup and broccoli. Top with teaspoonsful of Cheez Whiz. Bake at 350° about 1 hour and until cheese is melted.

CORN CASSEROLE

1 (4-oz.) can whole kernel corn
1 (4-oz. can cream style corn
1 egg
1 C. sour cream

½ C. margarine (melted)
1 small (8½-oz.) box corn
bread mix

Mix all ingredients together and bake at 350° for 45 minutes.

CORN PUDDING

2 eggs (beaten)
1 can cream style corn
5 T. flour

½ C. milk
Dash of salt and pepper
2 T. melted butter

Mix in order given. Bake at 325° for 1 hour.

BAKED BEANS

1 large (53-oz.) can pork and beans
1 T. mustard
1½ C. brown sugar
1 C. catsup

1 large onion (chopped)
1 small can crushed pineapple
5 strips bacon (diced)
2 T. vinegar

Mix all ingredients together and place in casserole dish and bake 20 minutes at 400°; then 45 minutes at 350°.

BAKED BEANS

1 (15-oz.) can pork and beans
¾ C. brown sugar
2 T. dark syrup

2 T. chopped onion
⅔ strip of bacon (cut up)
1 C. tomato juice

Mix all together. Bake covered at 350° for 1½ hours, then uncovered for ½ hour.

CARROT PUDDING

1 lb. carrots (boiled and peeled)	2 T. butter or margarine
1 loaf bread (crusts cut off)	6 eggs
2 C. milk	1 tsp. vanilla
1 C. sugar	1 T. flour

Wet bread in milk until soft. Place all ingredients in large bowl and mix with mixer until well blended. Pour into angel cake pan or mold and bake at 350° for 30-45 minutes. Serve as starch part of meal.

BROCCOLI CASSEROLE

1 large pkg. broccoli	½ C. Minute Rice
1 (8-oz.) jar of Cheese Whiz	¾ C. milk
1 can mushroom soup	

Combine all ingredients in a 2-qt. casserole. Bake covered for ½ hour at 350°. Bake uncovered for ½ hour at 350°.

BAKED CARROT CASSEROLE

4 C. carrots (cooked)
1 small onion
¼ C. butter or margarine

½ C. cheddar cheese (grated)
¾ C. corn flakes (crushed)

Slice carrots, cook. Place cooked carrots in a buttered casserole and cover with the following topping: Saute diced onion in melted butter or margarine; add grated cheese and crushed corn flakes. Put topping over carrots and bake for 30 minutes at 350°. Serves 6-8.

SCALLOPED CABBAGE

1 medium sized head cabbage
2 C. white sauce

Shredded cheese

Cut the cabbage into medium size pieces and cook until nearly done. Make white sauce. Put a layer of cabbage in a greased baking dish, cover with part of the white sauce. Then another layer of cabbage pieces. Cover with the rest of the white sauce and sprinkle shredded cheese on top of casserole. Bake in a 350° oven until mixture bubbles.

SPECIAL MASHED POTATOES

5 lbs. potatoes (cooked and mashed)
6-oz. cream cheese
1 C. sour cream

2 tsp. onion salt
¼ tsp. pepper
2 T. butter

Add softened cream cheese and other ingredients to mashed potatoes. Beat. Put in greased casserole for 30 minutes at 350°. This can be refrigerated up to 1½ weeks.

POTATOES SUPREME

1 (2-lb.) bag hash browns
½ C. melted butter
1 tsp. pepper
1 can cream of chicken soup
1 C. milk

½ pt. sour cream
2 C. grated cheddar cheese
2 C. crushed corn flakes
½ C. chopped onion

Place hash browns in a 9x13-inch metal cake pan. Sprinkle with salt and pepper. Put a layer of chopped onion over potatoes. Mix all remaining ingredients except flakes and butter. Pour over potatotes then top with corn flakes (which have been rolled in butter). Bake 60 minutes at 350°.

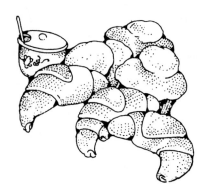

ZUCCHINI PIE

1 pkg. (8-oz.) crescent dinner rolls	½ tsp. pepper
4 C. (¼'' thick) cut pieces zucchini	½ tsp. garlic powder
1 C. chopped onion	¼ tsp. oregano
¼-½ C. margarine	2 eggs
½ C. chopped parsley (OR	8-oz. pkg. shredded mozzarella
2 T. parsley flakes	cheese
½ tsp. salt	2 tsp. mustard

Line 9-inch pie plate with 8-oz. crescent dinner rolls. Spread crust with 2 tsp. mustard. Cook zucchini, onion, and margarine for 5 minutes or until tender. Don't add water. Then stir in parsley flakes. Add salt, pepper, garlic powder, and oregano. Combine 2 eggs with 8-oz. pkg. cheese and add to vegetable mixture. Pour this mixture into crust and bake at 375° for 18-20 minutes or until center sets. Pie cuts better if you let it set 10 minutes after removing from oven.

SCALLOPED PINEAPPLE

20-oz. can crushed pineapple	1 C. grated cheese
(or tidbits)	(cheddar or longhorn)
1 c. sugar	½ C. soda cracker crumbs
2 T. flour	¼ C. margarine (melted)
¼ tsp. salt	

Mix pineapple, sugar, flour, salt and cheese. Spread in 8x8-inch baking dish. Top with mixed crumbs and margarine. Bake 350° for 35 minutes. Good with ham.

YOKKSHIRE PUDDING

¼ C. beef drippings
3 eggs
1 C. milk

1 C. all purpose flour
½ tsp. salt

Beat together the eggs and milk. Sift together the flour and salt and stir in egg mixture. Beat this batter until smooth. Preheat your pan and drippings in a pan at 450° for a few minutes, then pour your batter into the fat (don't stir it once it's in the pan) and bake at that temperature for 10-15 minutes. Now reduce the heat to 350° and bake another 10-15 minutes until puffy and brown. Serve in wedges or squares with the roast beef and gravy.

TWICE BAKED CHEESY POTATOES

4 medium baking potatoes
2 T. butter
½ C. sour cream
½ tsp. salt

1/8 tsp. pepper
½ C. shredded American cheese
2 T. thinly sliced green onion

Bake potatoes at 425° for 40-60 minutes. Cut a lengthwise slice from top of each potato. Scoop out insides leaving a ½-inch thick shell. Set shells aside. Mash potatoes; add butter, beat in sour cream. Add salt and pepper. Stir in cheese and onion. Spoon into shells. Cover and refrigerate 2-24 hours. Bake uncovered at 425° for 35 minutes or until lightly browned.

BREADS, ROLLS, ETC.

ALMOND TEA BREAD

2¼ C. sugar
3 eggs
1 C. + 2 T. oil
3 C. flour
1½ tsp. salt
1½ tsp. baking powder

1½ tsp. almond flavoring
1½ tsp. butter extract
1½ tsp. vanilla
1½ tsp. poppy seed
1½ C. milk

Cream sugar, eggs and oil. Sift together flour, salt, baking powder and add to above with the almond flavoring, butter extract, vanilla, poppy seed and milk. Put into greased and floured small loaf pans. Bake in a 350° oven 40-50 minutes. While still warm brush with following glaze: ¾ C. sugar, ¼ C. orange juice, ½ tsp. almond extract, ½ tsp. butter extract, ½ tsp. vanilla. Warm until sugar dissolves and brush on. Let stand until cool or overnight.

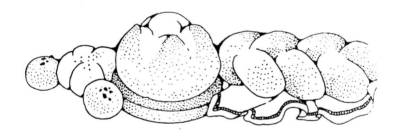

MONKEY BREAD

4 cans refrigerator biscuits
¾ C. sugar
1½ T.. cinnamon

¾ C. butter
¾ C. sugar
1½ T. cinnamon

Cut each biscuit into 4 pieces. In a large plastic bag or dish with a sealable lid, place ¾ C. sugar and 1½ T.cinnamon and the biscuit pieces and shake until all pieces are well coated. Place pieces into a well greased bundt or loaf pan. Bring to a boil the remaining ingredients. Pour over the biscuits. Bake at 350° for 30-40 minutes. Do Not Overbake.

DINNER ROLLS

2 pkg. yeast
1 C. warm water
1 tsp. sugar
2 C. warm milk
⅔ C. soft shortening

¾ C. sugar
4 tsp. salt
2 eggs (beaten)
10-11 C. flour

Dissolve yeast and 1 tsp. sugar in warm water. Add shortening, sugar, and salt. Mix in eggs; add milk and flour. Let rise until double in size. Make in rolls and let rise until double again. Bake at 400° for 15-20 minutes.

DOUGHNUTS

1 pkg. active dry yeast
¼ C. warm water
1 C. scalded milk
¼ C. shortening
¼ C. sugar

¾ C. mashed potatoes
(instant may be used)
2 eggs (beaten)
5-6 C. sifted flour
1 tsp. salt

GLAZE:
1 lb. powdered sugar
1 T. vanilla

6 T. water

Dissolve yeast in warm water. Combine milk, shortening, sugar and salt. Stir in the potatoes, eggs, and then yeast. Gradually add enough flour to make soft dough. Turn onto floured surface and knead until smooth and satiny. Place in greased bowl; turn over to grease top. Let stand in a warm place until double, 1-1½ hours. Roll to ½'' thickness; cut with 3-inch doughnut cutter. Let rise until double, about 30 minutes. Fry in deep fat (375°). Drain on paper towels.

For Glaze: Mix together powdered sugar, water and vanilla. Drop warm, drained doughnuts into glaze, then place on a rack to cool.

CHEESE-SAUSAGE QUICHE

¾ lb. sausage links
½ C. onion (chopped)
⅓ C. green pepper (chopped)
1½ C. sharp cheddar cheese (grated)
1 T. flour
1 (9-inch) deep-dish pie crust shell

2 eggs (beaten lightly)
1 C. evaporated milk
1 T. parsley flakes
¾ tsp. seasoned salt
¼ tsp. pepper
¼ tsp. garlic salt

Preheat oven to 375°. In medium skillet fry sausage until cooked. Remove sausage; drain on a paper towel. Reserve 2 T. fat; saute onion and green pepper in reserved fat for 2-3 minutes. Slice sausage into small pieces. Combine cheese and flour. Stir in sausage, green pepper and onion. Spread in pie shell. Mix remaining ingredients and pour into shell. Bake on a cookie sheet about 40 minutes. Serves 6.

BAKED FRENCH TOAST ALMONDINE

6 eggs
¼ C. liquid brown sugar
¼ C. milk

1 large loaf French bread
(¾-inch slices)
1 stick butter or margarine

SAUCE:
2 T. butter
1 C. sliced almonds

1½ C. liquid brown sugar
½ tsp. almond extract

With wire whisk, beat eggs, liquid brown sugar, and milk. Melt ½ butter in each of two 10x15-inch jelly roll pans. Remove pans from oven. Dip bread; place slices in single layers in pans. Bake in 450° oven for 10-15 minutes until golden. Turn bread occasionally. Serve with Almondine sauce.

For Sauce: Melt butter in pan; add almonds. Cook over moderate heat stirring until almonds are golden. Stir in brown sugar and extract.

HAM BREAKFAST SOUFFLE

2 T. butter
½ C. green pepper
½ C. onions (chopped)
16 slices bread
2 C. ham (cut in bite size pieces)
1 C. mushrooms (sliced)

4 C. cheddar cheese (shredded)
6 eggs
3 C. milk
1½ tsp. dry mustard
2 C. corn flakes (crushed)
1 T. butter

In a skillet saute pepper and onion in melted butter. Cut crust off bread. Place 8 slices of bread in bottom of 9x13-inch pan. Place ½ of cheese on top of bread. Layer in order the ham, sauteed vegetables and remaining cheese. Place remaining 8 slices of bread over top of all. Mix eggs, milk and mustard together. Pour over top of bread. If possible, let set a couple hours or overnight in refrigerator. Before baking, sprinkle with corn flakes and dabs of butter. Bake in 350° oven for 1½ hours or until set. Let stand 15 minutes, covered, prior to serving. Makes 12 servings.

PANCAKES

1¼ C. flour
3 tsp. baking powder
½ tsp. salt
3 tsp. sugar

1 egg (beaten)
2 T. oil
1 C. milk

Mix flour, baking powder, salt and sugar together. Mix in a bowl the egg, oil and milk. Add the two together to make batter.

74

FRENCH BREAKFAST PUFFS

⅓ C. soft shortening
½ C. sugar
1 egg
1½ C. flour
1½ tsp. baking powder

¼ tsp. nutmeg
½ C. milk
6 T. butter
½ C. sugar
1 tsp. cinnamon

Heat oven to 350°. Mix shortening, sugar, eggs. Sift dry ingredients; stir alternately with milk. Fill greased muffin tins ⅔ full. Bake 20-25 minutes until brown. Immediately roll in butter, then in mixture of sugar and cinnamon. Makes 12 medium sized puffs.

BREAKFAST PIZZA

1 lb. ground pork (browned)
1 pkg. (8-oz.) refrigerator
  crescent rolls
1 C. frozen hash browns (thawed)
1 C. cheddar cheese (shredded)
1 C. mozzarella cheese (shredded)
1 tsp. Presti pizza seasoning

¼ C. onion (chopped)
5 eggs
¼ C. milk
½ C. bacon crumbles
½ tsp. salt
½ C. mushrooms
2 T. parmesan cheese

Separate crescent rolls into 8 triangles. Place in ungreased 12-inch pizza pan, with points toward center. Press over bottom and up sides to form crust, sealing perforations. Spoon ground pork over crust, sprinkle with potatoes, bacon, onion, mushrooms and Presti seasoning. Top with cheeses. Beat eggs, milk and salt together. Pour into crust. Sprinkle parmesan cheese over all. Bake 25-30 minutes at 375°. Serves 6-8.

BUTTERMILK ROLLS - QUICK

4-4½ C. flour
2 pkg. yeast
3 T. sugar
1 tsp. salt

½ tsp. soda
1¼ C. buttermilk (I use powdered)
½ C. water
½ C. shortening

In a large mixer bowl, combine 1½ C. flour, yeast, sugar, salt and soda. Mix well. In saucepan heat buttermilk and shortening until warm. (Shortening does not need to melt.) Add to flour mixture. Blend at low speed until moistened, beat 3 minutes at medium speed. By hand, gradually add enough flour to make soft dough. Knead on floured surface until smooth and elastic, about 5 minutes. Let rise until double, about 20 minutes. Punch down and form into rolls. Cover and let rise until almost double, about 20 minutes. Bake at 400° 12-15 minutes until golden brown. Makes 24 rolls.

PIZZA DOUGH

1 pkg. yeast
1 tsp. sugar
2 T. salad oil

1 C. warm water
1 tsp. salt
2½ C. flour

Dissolve yeast in water. Stir in remaining ingredients, beat vigorously about 20 strokes. Allow dough to rest, about 5 minutes. On greased baking pan pat out ½ of the dough. Add pizza sauce and favorite topping of cheese and etc. Bake 425° 15-18 minutes. Makes 2 crusts.

BEST CINNAMON ROLLS

2 pkg. yeast	3 eggs
2½ C. warm water	⅓ C. oil
1 box yellow cake mix	1 tsp. salt
4½ C. flour	Margarine, sugar, cinnamon

Dissolve yeast in warm water for about 3 minutes. Add cake mix, 1 C. flour, eggs, oil, and salt. Beat with beater until bubbles appear. Add rest of the flour (3½ C.) slowly. Add more if too sticky. Stir until it forms a soft dough. Knead on flour board about 5 minutes. Let rise in bowl in warm place until double. Roll out ¼-inch. Spread with margarine, sugar and cinnamon. Roll up and cut. Place in greased pan. Let rise. Bake at 350° 20-30 minutes. Ice with powdered sugar glaze while hot.

BISCUITS

2 C. flour	2 tsp. sugar
4 tsp. baking powder	½ C. Crisco
½ tsp. salt	⅔ C. milk
½ tsp. cream of tartar	

Sift together dry ingredients. Cut in Crisco; add milk. Stir until dough follows fork around bowl. Turn out on lightly floured surface. Knead gently ½ minute. Pat or roll to ½''. Cut with biscuit cutter. Bake on ungreased cookie sheet at 450° for 10-12 minutes.

REFRIGERATOR BRAN MUFFINS

3 C. All Bran cereal (Nabisco)
1 C. water
2 C. buttermilk
2 eggs
½ C. oil

1 ½ C. sugar (part brown)
2 ½ C. sifted flour
2 ½ tsp. soda
1 C. raisins
or chopped dates (optional)

Mix cereal, water, and buttermilk and soak for 20 minutes. Beat in eggs and oil. Mix rest of ingredients separately then stir into bran mixture until well blended. Drop into greased muffin pan and bake at 375° for 12-13 minutes (Batter may be stored up to 2 weeks in refrigerator.)

SOUR CREAM COFFEE CAKE

1 C. margarine
1 C. sugar
3 eggs
1 tsp. vanilla
2 ½ C. flour

2 tsp. baking powder
1 tsp. soda
½ tsp. salt
1 C. sour cream

TOPPING:
¾ C. brown sugar
2 tsp. cinnamon

½ C. nuts
½ C. coconut (optional)

Mix topping ingredients together. Cream together margarine and sugar. Add eggs; mix well. Add dry ingredients, then add sour cream. Place ½ of batter in greased 9x13-inch pan. Sprinkle with ⅓ of the topping. Add rest of batter. Put on rest of topping. Bake 375° for 30 minutes.

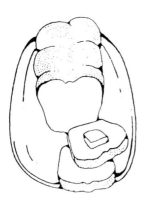

PUMPKIN BREAD

3 C. sugar
4 eggs
1 tsp. cinnamon
⅔ C. cold water
3½ C. flour
2 tsp. soda (mix with flour)

1 C. shortening
½ tsp. salt
1 tsp. nutmeg
2 C. pumpkin (1 No. 2 size can)
Nuts (opt.)

Mix all ingredients together. Bake at 350° for 1 hour or until done. Makes 3 small loaves or 2 large. I also make muffins with this recipe and bake 20 minutes in cupcake papers.

PECAN BREAD

2½ C. all purpose flour
1¼ C. sugar
1 tsp. salt
2 tsp. baking powder

2 C. chopped pecans
2 large eggs or 3 small eggs
1 C. + 1 T. milk

Sift the dry ingredients into large bowl and then add the pecans. In another bowl vigorously beat the eggs and when they are thick and frothy, add the milk. Stir the beaten egg mixture into the dry ingredients. Pour the batter into a well-greased 8x4-inch loaf pan. Bake in a preheated 350° oven for 1 hour. Remove from the pan and let cool on a wire rack. Yields 1 loaf.

CINNAMON BREAD

1 yellow cake mix
1 pkg. instant vanilla pudding
4 eggs
¾ C. oil

¾ C. water
¼ C. sugar
2 tsp. cinnamon

Beat cake mix, pudding, eggs, oil, and water for 8 minutes. Pour ½ of the batter in bread loaf pan. Sprinkle with ⅔ of the sugar and cinnamon mixture. Pour on remaining batter and top with remaining sugar. Bake in a 325° oven for 45-50 minutes.

ONE PAN CRANBERRY BREAD

¼ C. vegetable oil
½ C. dairy sour cream
¼ C. milk
3 eggs
2⅓ C. Bisquick baking mix

¾ C. sugar
2 T. grated orange peel
¾ C. chopped fresh or
   frozen cranberries
½ C. chopped nuts

Heat oven to 375°. Generously grease bottom of 9x5x3-inch loaf pan. Stir all ingredients except cranberries and nuts in pan with fork until moistened; beat vigorously 1 minute. Stir in cranberries and nuts. Bake until wooden pick inserted in center comes out clean, 50-55 minutes. Cool 5 minutes. Run knife or metal spatula around sides of loaf to loosen; remove from pan. If desired, cool loaf completely and drizzle with glaze (below). Makes 1 loaf.

For Glaze: Beat ½ C. powdered sugar and 2-3 tsp. orange juice until smooth and of desired consistency.

GLAZED APPLE BREAD

½ C. shortening
1 C. sugar
2 T. milk
1 tsp. vanilla
2 eggs
2 C. flour

1 tsp. cinnamon
2½ tsp. baking powder
¼ tsp. salt
¼ C. nuts (chopped)
1 C. unpared apples
   (finely chopped)

Cream first 4 ingredients, add eggs and beat well. Sift flour, baking powder, cinnamon and salt and add to above; also add apples and nuts. Stir until flour is well dampened. Pour into oiled bread pan. Bake at 350° for 50-60 minutes. Remove from pan and pour glaze over loaf letting it drip down the sides. Allow glaze to set, then wrap tightly. For better flavor make bread a day or two before you use it.

APPLE   BREAD   GLAZE:
½ C. powdered sugar (sifted)   1 T. water
2 T. butter or margarine (melted) ½ T. cinnamon

BANANA BREAD

2 med. sized bananas (ripe, mashed)
1 egg
1 C. sugar
2 tsp. butter (melted)
1 tsp. salt

½ C. sour milk
1 tsp. soda, dissolved in sour milk
2 C. flour
1 tsp. vanilla

Mix in order given. Bake in loaf pan that is well greased and floured. Bake 350° for 35-40 minutes or until done in the center.

MEATS & MAIN DISHES

GREEN PEPPER STEAK

1 lb. beef chuck or round
(with fat trimmed)
¼ C. soy sauce
1 clove garlic
½ tsp. ground ginger
¼ C. salad oil
1 C. onion (chopped)

1 C. red or green peppers
(cut into 1-inch squares)
2 stalks celery (thinly sliced)
1 T. cornstarch
1 C. water
2 tomatoes (cut into wedges)

Cut beef into cubes or thin strips. Combine soy sauce, garlic, and ginger. Add beef. Toss and set aside while preparing vegetables. Heat oil in large frying pan or wok. Add beef and toss over high heat until browned. Cover and simmer over low heat until tender, 20-30 minutes. Turn up heat and add vegetables. Toss until vegetables are tender crisp, about 10 minutes. Mix cornstarch with water. Add to pan; stir and cook until thickened. Add tomatoes and heat through. If desired, you may prepare the beef and marinade ahead of time and refrigerate.

BEERY BEEF STEW

¼ C. flour
1 tsp. salt
½ tsp. pepper
2 lbs. stew meat (cubed)
½ C. olive oil
2 lbs. onions (peeled and sliced)
1 clove garlic (crushed)
1 giant-size can beer
1 T. soy sauce

1 T. Worcestershire sauce
1 T. steak sauce
½ tsp. crumbled bay leaves
1 tsp. dried thyme
2 lbs. potatoes
(pared and quartered)
4 medium carrots (in chunks)
Boiling water
Parsley

Coat the cubed meat in the flour which has been mixed with salt and pepper; set aside. In a large pot, heat ¼ C. of the olive oil and saute the onion and garlic until tender, about 5 minutes. Remove onion from pot; add the remaining oil. Heat and add the floured meat, browning it well on all sides. Return the onion-garlic mixture along with the beer, the 3 sauces, and the herbs. Mix well; bring mixture to a boil. Reduce heat; cover and simmer for 1 hour and 30 minutes. Add the pared, quartered potatoes to the stew with just enough boiling water to make enough juice for them to cook in. After about 15 minutes, add the carrots. In another 20 minutes or so, when potatoes are tender, you are ready to serve. Sprinkle some parsley on top just before carrying the pot to the table. Makes 4-6 servings.

CHICKEN WITH BROCCOLI AND CAULIFLOWER

2 chicken breasts
1 large pkg. frozen broccoli
and cauliflower
1 can chicken or mushroom soup

⅓ C. mayonnaise
1½ tsp. lemon juice
1 tsp. curry powder
¼-½ lb. Velveeta cheese

Cook and bone 2 chicken breasts. Cook 1 large package of frozen broccoli and cauliflower in small amount of water until crisp tender. Drain. (Save liquid for soup or other vegetables.) Put in oblong baking dish, cut in chicken in bite-size pieces and put on top of vegetables. In double boiler mix: 1 can chicken or mushroom soup (do not dilute); ⅓ C. mayonnaise; 1½ tsp. lemon juice; 1 tsp. curry powder; ¼-½ lb. Velveeta cheese. Heat until cheese is melted. Pour over chicken and vegetables. Top with buttered bread crumbs. Bake 45 minutes in a 350° oven or until hot and bubbly. (This may be frozen ahead of time. Allow extra time for thawing if frozen. This recipe may be doubled very easily.)

CORN DOGS

1 lb. hot dogs
¾ C. self-rising flour
¼ C. corn meal
1 T. sugar
Popsicle sticks

2 T. dry onion soup mix
1 egg
½ C. milk
1 tsp. dry mustard

Beat egg and milk together. Add to all the dry ingredients to make a batter. Insert sticks into hot dogs that are wiped dry and dusted with flour. Dip these into the batter and cook in hot (375°) oil, cooking until brown. Drain on paper towels. Serve hot.

BAKED RABBIT

1 wild rabbit
Flour, salt, pepper

1 C. whipping cream

Soak wild rabbit for 12-24 hours in strong salt water. Dip in flour, salt and pepper to taste. Brown in oil. Place in casserole. Add 1 C. whipping cream, cover and bake 325°-350° until tender. (Cream takes wild taste away.)

SWEET SOUR PORK

1½ lb. pork shoulder
2 T. oil
½ C. water
15½-oz. can pineapple chunks
2 T. cornstarch
¼ C. brown sugar

⅓ C. vinegar
1 T. soy sauce
¾ green pepper
¼ C. thinly sliced onion
½ tsp. salt

Brown pork cubed in hot skillet. Add water and simmer covered 1 hour until tender. Drain pineapple, reserving juice. Add water if necessary to make 1 C. Combine cornstarch, salt and brown sugar. Blend in vinegar; stir in reserved pineapple juice and soy sauce. Cook stirring constantly until thickened and bubbly. Pour sauce over hot pork and let stand 10 minutes. Add green pepper, onion and pineapple chunks. Simmer covered 2-3 minutes or until vegetables are tender. Serve over cooked rice. Serves 4.

NOODLE AND TUNA CASSEROLE

¼ C. onion (chopped)
1 can tuna
2 T. fat
1 can cream of mushroom soup

1 C. milk
½ tsp. salt
3 C. noodles (cooked)

Cook onion and tuna in the fat until onion is soft. Stir in mushroom soup, milk, salt and noodles. Bake in casserole topped with ½ C. buttered bread crumbs at 375° for 15 minutes.

TUNA AND RICE

1 C. tuna
1 C. rice (cooked)
2 hard-boiled eggs

Salt
Pepper

Add a little butter and some cream and mix all together.

PORK CHOP 'N POTATO BAKE

6 pork chops
Vegetable oil
Durkey seasoned salt
1 can cream of celery soup
½ C. milk
½ C. sour cream

¼ tsp. pepper
1 (24-oz.) pkg. frozen hash
  browns (thawed)
1 C. shredded cheddar cheese
1 can (small) onion rings

Brown pork chops in lightly greased skillet. Sprinkle with seasoned salt and set aside. Combine soup, milk, sour cream, pepper, and ½ tsp. seasoned salt. Stir in potatoes, ½ C. cheese and ½ can onion rings. Spoon mixture into 9x13-inch baking dish. Arrange pork chops over potatoes. Bake, covered at 350° for 40 minutes. Top with remaining cheese and onion rings; bake, uncovered 5 minutes longer.

ORANGE-HAM ROLL UPS

1 can (11-oz.) mandarin oranges
  (chopped and drained)
1½ C. cooked rice (white or wild)
⅓ C. mayonnaise

2 T. chopped pecans
2 T. parsley flakes
2 T. chopped onion
8 slices ham (sliced thin)

Combine oranges, rice, mayonnaise, parsley and onion. Divide into 8 portions and place on ham slices. Roll up ham and place seam-side down in baking dish. Then combine: ¼ C. orange marmalade, 1 T. lemon juice, and ¼ tsp. ground ginger. Pour over ham rolls and bake at 350° for 25-30 minutes, uncovered.

CHICKEN WINGS . . . BUFFALO STYLE

2½ lbs. chicken wings (12-15 wings)   ½ C. butter or margarine
¼ C. Red Hot

Split wings at each joint and discard tips; pat dry. Deep fry at 400° for 12 minutes or until completely cooked and crispy; drain. Combine hot sauce and butter. Dip wings in sauce to coat completely. Serve with celery and blue cheese dip. (For equally crispy wings, bake on a rack or in a roasting pan at 425° for 1 hour. Turn halfway through cooking time.)

SWEET AND SOUR STEW

½ lb. stew meat   1 (8-oz.) can tomato soup
2 T. cooking oil   ¼ C. brown sugar
1 C. carrots (cut up)   1/8 C. or less vinegar
1 C. onion slices   1 T. Worcestershire sauce

Brown meat in hot oil. Add next 6 ingredients, and ½ C. water. Cover and cook at 350° until meat is tender, about 3½ hours. May be cooked in a crock pot on low heat for 8 hours. May be served over rice or noodles.

90

BARBECUED SPARE RIBS

4 lb. spare ribs
1 C. diced onion
1 C. catsup or chili sauce
1 C. water
2 tsp. salt

2 tsp. Worcestershire sauce
½ C. vinegar
¼ C. brown sugar
2 tsp. dry mustard
½ tsp. chili powder

Mix all of the ingredients and pour over spare ribs. Bake in oven for 1¾ hours at 350°. Bake uncovered the last 15 minutes.

SUMMER SAUSAGE

2 lbs. lean hamburger
1 C. water
2 T. liquid smoke

2 T. salt
¼ tsp. garlic powder
¼ tsp. onion powder

Mix together well and shape into 2 long loaves. Wrap in foil with the shiny side to meat. Refrigerate for 24 hours. Bake for 90 minutes in a 350° oven. Bake on cookie sheets to keep oven clean. Let cool, slice and eat. Great for snacks.

BARBECUE BEEF SANDWICHES

5 lb. roast (chuck)   2 T. Worcestershire sauce
1 small bottle catsup   Pinch of salt
1 qt. 7-Up

Pour ingredients over roast and put in oven. Bake 300° for 7 hours. Stir occasionally. It should be in a covered roaster.

HAM MEATBALLS

1 lb. ground ham mix   ½ C. milk
½ lb. ground beef   1 C. bread crumbs
2 eggs   1 small onion (optional)

GLAZE:
1 C. brown sugar   2 T. mustard
⅓ C. vinegar

Mix all ingredients well and make into large meatballs. Mix glaze ingredients and boil 1 minute. Pour over meatballs just before going into the oven. Baste meatballs with glaze 3 times during baking. This can also be made into a loaf, also basting 3 times.

TACO PIE

1½ lbs. ground beef
1 envelope dry taco mix
1 pkg. crescent dinner rolls

1 C. sour cream
1 C. grated cheddar cheese

Brown beef; add taco mix and water as directed on package. Mix and simmer 5 minutes. Line 9 or 10-inch greased pie pan with crescent dough. Fill with beef mixture. Spread with sour cream and top with cheese. Bake at 350° about 20 minutes. Top with lettuce.

GROUND BEEF STROGANOFF

1 lb. ground beef
1 small onion (chopped)
½ tsp. instant beef bouillon

1 can cream of mushroom soup
½ can water
½ C. sour cream

Brown beef and onion; stir in other ingredients. Cook over low heat, stirring occasionally for 15-20 minutes. Serve over rice or noodles.

FOOTBALL CHILI

1 can tomatoes	1 can kidney beans
1 onion	Chili seasoning
Hamburger	Salt

Men can do this while they watch the game on TV. Put a can of tomatoes, the chopped onion and a ''double handful'' of hamburger into a large skillet or pan. Place over slow fire, then break up lumps and stir during commercials. At halftime add a can of kidney beans, chili powder and salt. Let simmer until game is over. It will be ready for supper.

POOR MAN'S PIZZA

2 lbs. ground beef	¼ - ½ tsp. oregano
¼ C. oil	8-oz. mozzarella cheese
¼ tsp. garlic salt	10¾-oz. tomato soup
Salt and pepper	

Brown meat; salt and pepper to taste. Cool and drain off fat. Add to cooled meat the cheese, oil, garlic salt, oregano and tomato soup. Spread this mixture on hamburger bun halves and lay on broiler pan and broil until cheese is bubbly and hot. For best results leave the oven rack in the position as you usually bake a cake.

CHEESY SPAGHETTI CASSEROLE

1 lb. hamburger
1 small onion
6-oz. spaghetti
1 can spaghetti sauce
2 T. butter

4 tsp. flour
¾ C. Carnation evaporated milk
⅓ C. water
1 C. shredded mozzarella cheese
2 T. parmesan cheese

Prepare spaghetti sauce and prepare spaghetti. Melt butter and stir in flour and salt. Slowly add milk and water and cook over medium heat, stirring constantly until thickened. Add ½ C. shredded cheese and all parmesan cheese. Put ½ spaghetti mixture in 9x13-inch pan. Pour over all the sauce. Top with remaining spaghetti. Sprinkle ½ C. grated cheese on top. Bake 350° for 45 minutes.

POPOVER PIZZA

1 lb. hamburger
1 small onion
½ tsp. salt
1 (15½-oz.) can pizza sauce
1 (8-oz.) pkg. mozzarella cheese
Green pepper

Pepperoni or sausage
2 eggs
1 C. milk
1 tsp. vegetable oil
1 C. flour
¼ C. parmesan cheese

Brown and drain the hamburger, onion, and salt. Add the pizza sauce and spread in 9x13-inch pan. Sprinkle with the mozzarella cheese. Mix together the eggs, milk, oil and flour and pour over meat and cheese. Top with the parmesan cheese and bake at 400° for 30 minutes.

SIMPLE LASAGNA

1 (8-oz.) box lasagna noodles
1 lb. ground beef
⅓ C. chopped onion
2 large cans tomato sauce
1 tsp. Italian seasonings

1 tsp. garlic powder
½ tsp. leaf oregano
½ tsp. parsley flakes
4 C. mozzarella cheese

Brown hamburger with onions; salt and pepper to taste. Drain and add tomato sauce and seasonings. Bring to a boil then cover and simmer for 20 minutes. Cook lasagna as directed, then drain. In well greased 9x13-inch baking dish, layer noodles, sauce, and cheese 3 times. Bake at 350° for 30 minutes. Let set 10 minutes before serving.

MEAL-IN-ONE

1½ lb. hamburger
6 medium potatoes (peeled and sliced)
1 carrot (shredded)

1 small onion
1 can whole kernel corn (drained)
  or 1 pkg. frozen corn

Slightly cook hamburger, drain off grease. Salt and pepper to taste. In alternate layers, put potatoes, carrot, corn and onions. Cook at 260° (steam). Steam cook this for about 1 hour, turning occasionally. This cooks best in an electric skillet. Can also be baked in the oven, except do not drain off the grease.

MANICOTTI

1½ lb. ground beef (saute with onion
   and drain excess fat)
1 C. bread crumbs
1 T. chopped parsley
8-oz. grated mozzarella cheese
1 tsp. pepper
1 tsp. salt

2 eggs (slightly beaten)
1 C. cottage cheese
   (slightly beaten)
½ C. milk
12-14 manicotti shells
4 C. spaghetti sauce

Add the cooked beef to the rest of the ingredients and stuff into 12-14 cooked manicotti shells. Place filled shells in a single layer in greased baking dish. Pour 2 C. spaghetti sauce over manicotti. Cover and bake 350° for 25-35 minutes. Before serving add 2 more cups heated spaghetti sauce. You may sprinkle with parmesan cheese. Serves 2 shells per person.

FIX AND FORGET CASSEROLE

1 lb. lean hamburger
¾ C. raw rice
1 can mixed vegetables (not drained)

1 pkg. dry onion soup
1 can celery soup
1 can beef consomme

Mix all together and bake at 325° for 3 hours.

GUINEA GRINDERS

1 lb. hamburger
1 lb. Italian hot sausage
1 onion (chopped)

Salt and pepper to taste
1 can pizza sauce
1 loaf French bread

Cook meats and onion and drain off fat. Add pizza sauce. Cut lengthwise 1 loaf French bread, put in filling and cover with 1 pkg. mozzarella cheese. Wrap in foil and bake 15-20 minutes at 350°. Slice and serve.

HAMBURGER CASSEROLE

1 lb. ground beef
1 C. onion (chopped)
1 C. celery
1 pkg. frozen peas
1 can mushroom soup

1 can cream of chicken soup
1 soup can of water
½ C. raw rice
¼ C. soy sauce
¼ tsp. pepper

Brown ground beef, then add rest of ingredients. Put in 2½-qt. casserole; cover. Bake at 350° for 30 minutes. Remove cover and bake just a few minutes. Don't cook too long.

POTATO COVERED MEAT LOAF

Instant potatoes   Brown gravy

Prepare meat loaf as usual and cook as usual. Depending on the size of your meatloaf fix enough instant potatoes to cover the meat loaf. After the meat is cooked, drain well. Spread on your prepared potatoes. Sprinkle some paprika on top and put in oven until brown. Prepare a brown gravy and serve over meatloaf.

ITALIAN MEAT LOAF

¾ C. cracker crumbs   ¼ C. chopped onion
1 C. milk   1 T. Worcestershire sauce
1 ½ lb. ground chuck   ½ tsp. salt
2 eggs   ½ tsp. garlic salt
½ C. grated romano cheese   ¼ tsp. basil
¼ C. minced green pepper   Dash of pepper

Soak cracker crumbs and milk. Add rest of ingredients. Put in pan. Spread catsup over loaf. Sprinkle with small amount of additional romano cheese and basil. Bake 350° for 45 minutes. Delicious and "spoonable".

SWEDISH MEATBALLS

1 ¼ lb. hamburger
¾ C. quick oatmeal
1 C. milk

3 T. minced onion
1 ½ tsp. salt
¼ tsp. pepper

SAUCE:
2 C. catsup
1 C. water

2 T. Worcestershire sauce
1 T. minced onion

Mix and make into small balls. Brown in hot shortening. Put in baking dish. Make a sauce from above ingredients. Let sauce simmer 10 minutes. Pour over meatballs in a baking dish. Bake 350° for 30 minutes.

PIZZA MEATLOAF

2 lbs. ground beef or turkey
1 C. cracker crumbs
½ C. chopped onion
2 eggs (beaten)
1 (8-oz.) can pizza sauce

1 tsp. salt
½ C. parmesan cheese
¼ tsp. oregano
1 C. milk
1 C. shredded mozzarella cheese

Mix meat, eggs, onion, crumbs, spices, milk and parmesan cheese. Put into an 8-inch square pan and bake at 350° for 45 minutes. Spread sauce over meat and top with mozzarella cheese. Return to oven for 8-10 minutes or until done.

MEAT LOAF

1 lb. ground chuck
1 lb. sausage
1 C. sour cream
1 envelope onion soup mix

1 C. bread crumbs
Salt
Pepper

Combine above ingredients. Bake at 350° for 2 hours.

MEAT BALLS

2 lbs. hamburger
1 C. Eagle Brand milk
½ tsp. salt

¾ C. oatmeal
1 tsp. minced onion
¼ tsp. pepper

SAUCE:
2 T. sugar
2 T. vinegar
2 C. catsup

2 T. Worcestershire sauce
1 C. water
¼ tsp. minced onion

Form the mixture into balls. Stir sauce and pour over balls. Cover with foil. Bake 2 hours in a 300° oven.

MEATBALLS

3 lb. ground chuck
4 slices bread
¼ tsp. nutmeg
2 tsp. garlic salt
¼ tsp. pepper

¼ tsp. allspice
¾ C. milk
Chopped onion
2 eggs

Mix above ingredients. Let stand to absorb flavors. Shape in walnut-size balls. Barely brown. Place in single layer in baking pan. Cover with 1 C. bouillon (1 cube in 1 C. hot water). Add Open Pit barbecue sauce to taste. Bake 350° for about 30 minutes.

LOW CALORIE HOT DISH

1 small head cabbage
1 lb. hamburger
1 small onion (chopped)

¼ C. uncooked rice
1 can tomato soup
1 can water

Brown meat and onions, drain off fat; add rice and mix well with cabbage that is cut in ½-inch squares, put in greased casserole dish and pour tomato soup and water that has been heated through. Bake 1½ hours at 350°.

HEARTY HODGEPODGE

1½-2 lbs. ground beef
¾ C. onion (chopped)
2 T. powdered garlic
3 cans condensed minestrone soup
1½ C. celery (chopped)

3 (1-lb.) cans or 1 (30-oz.) can
    pork and beans
1 T. Worcestershire sauce
½-¾ tsp. oregano
½ tsp. basil

In large pan or skillet cook beef, onion, celery and garlic. Drain grease when meat is brown and celery and onion tender. Stir in soup, 3 cans water, oregano, beans and Worcestershire sauce. Simmer covered 15-20 minutes until flavors mix. Makes 12-14 servings. Excellent for a large crowd of teenagers after games. Cool and freeze in plastic containers if desired.

PIZZA DOUGH AND SAUCE

DOUGH:
7-oz. cold water
1 pkg. dry yeast
1½ tsp. sugar

1½ tsp. salt
3 C. flour
3 T. olive oil

SAUCE:
1 (8-oz.) tomato paste
1 (8-oz.) tomato sauce
1/8-¼ tsp. thyme
¼ tsp. ground rosemary
¼-½ tsp. caraway seed

¼ tsp. oregano
1 clove garlic or
    ¼ tsp. minced garlic
1 bay leaf

For Dough: Mix well, knead 5 minutes; let rise 1 hour. Makes 2 12-inch pizza crusts. Bake at 400°-500° 15-20 minutes.

For Sauce: Mix ingredients together and simmer. Cool slightly.

For Toppings: 1-1½ lbs. meat, ½ lb. mozzarella cheese and ½ lb. monterey jack cheese.

TACO BAKE

1½-2 lbs. ground beef	2 T. flour
1 small onion (finely chopped)	2 T. vinegar
1 clove garlic (chopped)	2 T. chili powder
3 (8-oz.) cans tomato sauce	1 C. grated cheddar cheese
1½ C. water	1 pkg. taco shells
1 small can sliced olives (drained)	

In small amount of oil, brown ground beef, onion and garlic; drain off fat and add tomato sauce, water, olives, flour, vinegar and chili powder. Simmer for 10 minutes. Butter an oblong baking dish and layer meat sauce and taco shells, beginning and ending with the meat sauce. Sprinkle grated cheese over top and bake in a 350° oven for 45 minutes. Let stand 10 minutes and serve. Serve with green salad and your favorite cheap red wine. Good company dish and a family favorite.

SILVER DOLLAR STEAKS

1 lb. 75-80 percent lean ground pork	¼ C. bread crumbs
1 tsp. salt	1 T. onion flakes
¼ tsp. pepper	1 T. dried mixed vegetables (opt.)
1 egg	1 can cream of chicken soup

Beat egg; add remaining ingredients except soup and vegetables. Shape into 4 flattened steaks. Pour soup over steaks. Sprinkle dried mixed vegetables on top of soup. Bake 1 hour at 350°. Serves 4. Variation: Substitute 1 can of any cream soup for chicken soup.

FRENCH DIP SANDWICHES

3-4 lb. roast
3-4 bouillon cubes

3 C. water
1 pkg. dry onion soup mix

Cook 3-4 lb. roast long and slow; cut or pull into pieces. Mix with 3-4 bouillon cubes, 3 C. water and 1 pkg. dry onion soup mix. Simmer 1 hour. Serve on hard rolls with juices for dip.

SPICEY SUMMER SAUSAGE

1½ lbs. ground beef (lean)
½ lb. ground pork
4 T. Morton's Tender Quick
½ tsp. garlic powder
1½ tsp. charcoal smoke salt

Dash of nutmeg
1 C. water
½ tsp. celery seed
1 tsp. Italian seasoning

Mix all ingredients together and form into 4 rolls each 2-inches in diameter. Seal each roll in aluminum foil and refrigerate 24 hours. Place rolls (still wrapped) in large pan, cover with water and boil 1 hour. Open the foil and drain. Cool. Wrap each roll in plastic wrap and refrigerate. (Optional: Whole peppercorns or whole mustard seed may be added before wrapping to store. These freeze well.)

CHIPPED BEEF CASSEROLE

1 C. shell macaroni
1 can cream of mushroom soup
1 C. milk
¼ C. minced onion

1 C. shredded sharp
  cheddar cheese
1 (4-oz.) pkg. chipped beef
  (snipped fine)

Place 1 C. dry (uncooked) shell macaroni in a buttered baking dish. Mix rest of ingredients and pour mixture over macaroni. Do not stir. Cover and place in refrigerator for 6-8 hours or overnight. When ready to bake, take a spoon and go to the bottom of the casserole in several places without stirring. Bake 1 hour at 350°.

STEW

1 can stew (Dinty Moore, etc.)
1 can corned beef

1 can pork and beans
Onion(diced)

Brown onion in bacon grease; add corned beef, heating just enough to break up. Add stew the same way; next the beans. Heat and cook for 20-30 minutes, simmering. Great reheated.

LASAGNE

1 lb. hamburger	1 qt. jar Ragu
½ lb. sausage (optional)	1 (24-oz.) lowfat cottage cheese
Onion	4 slices Swiss cheese
2 (15-oz.) cans tomato sauce	1 pkg. (8-oz.) mozzarella cheese
1 (15-oz.) can water	1 (16-oz.) pkg. lasagne noodles
1 pkg. spaghetti sauce mix	

Brown meats and onion; pour off fat. While doing this simmer tomato sauce, water, spaghetti sauce and Ragu. Cook noodles. Mix drained cottage cheese with other cheeses. Add sauce mixture to meat. In big greased 9x13-inch pan start with meat mixture, then noodles, then cheese mixture, ending with meat sauce. Sprinkle parmesan on top. Bake at 325° for 45 minutes.

WESTERN CHILI CASSEROLE

1 lb. hamburger	2 cans chili with beans
¾ C. chopped onion	½ tsp. pepper
¼ C. chopped celery	2 C. corn chips (crushed)
1 C. grated cheese	1 pt. taco sauce or tomato sauce

Brown hamburger, onion and celery; drain. Add rest of ingredients, but only 1 C. corn chips. Put in a 9x13-inch pan and sprinkle the remaining cup of corn chips on the top. Bake 45 minutes at 350°.

SHEPHERDS PIE

1 ½ lbs. ground beef
½ C. celery
1 onion
1 T. green pepper

2 cans vegetable soup
2 C. mashed potatoes
Salt, pepper and paprika

Brown and drain ground beef. Add celery, onion and green pepper. Mix all with soup and put ingredients in casserole. Cover with the mashed potatoes. Bake at 350° for 30 minutes. You can use instant potatoes.

NEAR EAST CASSEROLE

1 lb. hamburger
¼ C. dry bread crumbs
2 T. milk
¼ tsp. salt
2 T. margarine

1 can mushroom roup
1 can onion soup
1 can of water
½ C. rice (uncooked)

Combine the hamburger, crumbs, milk and salt. Shape into 18 balls and brown in margarine. Add the mushroom and onion soup and water. Bring to a boil and add the rice. Simmer for 25 minutes in large skillet.

BEANS

1 (15½-oz.) can red kidney beans
1 (15½-oz.) can butter beans
2 (15½-oz.) cans pork and beans
½ lb. bacon (crumbled after
  being cooked)
1 lb. raw hamburger

1 onion (chopped)
½ C. white sugar
¾ C. brown sugar
½ C. catsup
1 T. mustard (dry or salad)
2 tsp. vinegar

Mix all ingredients together and bake at 350° for 1 hour or in slow crock pot longer.

HAMBURGER AND DRESSING

1 lb. hamburger (cooked and drained)
2 C. dry bread crumbs
1 egg
1 C. milk

1 T. sage
Salt and pepper to taste
1 C. chicken and noodle soup

Mix all ingredients together and put in a buttered casserole dish and bake at 350°
35-40 minutes.

EASY OVEN STEW

2 lbs. stew meat
¼ C. flour
2 tsp. salt
¼ tsp. pepper
2 T. oil
4 small onions (quartered)

4 small carrots (cut in pieces)
4 small potatoes (halved)
1 C. celery (sliced)
1 C. water
2 (8-oz.) cans tomato sauce
with mushrooms

Combine flour, salt, pepper in a paper bag. Drop in beef, portion at a time, shake until coated. Mix with oil in a 3-qt. casserole. Bake uncovered at 400° for 30 minutes; stir once. Add vegetables, water and sauce. Mix well, cover and bake at 350° for 1¾ hour or until done. Serves 6.

FLANK STEAK PINWHEELS

1½ lbs. flank steak (trimmed)
1 bottle (1-lb.) barbecue sauce with
onions and meat tenderizer

3 whole dill pickles

Brush one side of steak with barbecue sauce. Place row of dill pickles lengthwise down center of steak. Roll steak tightly lengthwise. Tie with cord in several places. Place steak in shallow dish; coat well with barbecue sauce. Cover; refrigerate at least 15 minutes. (1 hour is best.) Prepare outdoor grill or preheat broiler. Place steak on cutting board. Insert skewers cross-wise through meat and pickles, about 1½ inches apart. Slice evenly between skewers to make pinwheels. Grill or broil on rack about 4 inches from medium-high coals 5-7 minutes on each side (or until as done as you like), basting frequently with barbecue sauce. Heat remaining barbecue sauce, serve with pinwheels. Makes 6 servings.

PEPPER STEAK

2 lbs. cubed beef (steak or roast)
1 (4-oz.) can mushrooms
  or 8-oz. fresh mushrooms
1 medium onion (chopped)

1 green pepper (chopped)
½ C. soy sauce
1 can bean sprouts

Brown meat; if using roast, simmer in water to make tender. Add onions and fry until tender, about 2 minutes. Add pepper and fry about 2 more mintues. Add soy sauce and mushrooms, fry for 1 minute. Add bean sprouts and heat through, 2 minutes. Serve with rice and soy sauce to taste.

MEAT PIE

4 T. cooking fat
3 T. chopped onion
2 T. chopped green pepper
½ C. diced celery
1 C. diced cooked meat

4 T. flour
2 C. milk or meat stock
½ C. diced, cooked carrots
Biscuits

Slowly brown onion, pepper, celery and meat in fat, stirring constantly. Add flour slowly, stirring constantly, until lightly brown. Add remaining ingredients. Heat thoroughly. Pour into shallow well-oiled baking dish. Cover with biscuits and bake in a hot oven (450°) about 15 minutes. Serves 6.

BAKED MEAT BALLS

MEATBALLS:
1½ lb. ground beef   ¾ C. oatmeal
1 C. milk   Salt and pepper to taste

SAUCE:
1 C. water   1 T. sugar
1 T. Worcestershire sauce   ¾ C. catsup
1 T. vinegar   Onion to taste (chopped)

Combine ingredients for meatballs (any size you want). Prepare sauce and bring to boil and pour over meatballs. Bake 350° oven for at least 1 hour. (I baked for 1½ hours.) Uncovered last 15 minutes. Spoon sauce over meatballs during baking time.

KOREAN SUN PORK

1 can pineapple chunks   2 large cloves garlic
3 T. soy sauce   2 T. minced ginger root
1 T. cornstarch   or 1 tsp. ground ginger
1 tsp. white vinegar   1 onion (quartered)
½ tsp. hot red pepper flakes   2 medium carrots (slivered)
1 lb. boneless pork roast   1 green bell pepper (slivered)
2 T. vegetable oil

Drain pineapple, reserve 3 T. juice. Mix reserved juice with water (½ C.); soy sauce, cornstarch, vinegar and pepper flakes; set aside. Cut pork in strips. In skillet, brown pork in hot oil. Add garlic and ginger; cook 1 minute. Add onion and carrots; cook 1 minute. Stir sauce; add to skillet with pineapple and bell pepper. Cook until sauce boils and thickens. Serves 4.

OVEN FRIED CHICKEN

1 3-lb. chicken (cut up)

Combine these 3 ingredients in bag and shake:
½ C. bread crumbs   2 T. oil
½ C. parmesan cheese

Then add:
1 tsp. salt   ½ tsp. pepper
½ tsp. basil   ½ tsp. garlic powder

and shake again.

Then add the cut-up chicken and shake to coat chicken. Arrange in pan with thicker pieces to outside and wings, etc. in middle. Gizzards may be placed under other pieces of chicken. Again, bake 9 minutes per lb. or 27 minutes. You may add cream of mushroom soup halfway through for variety. Also you may use cracker crumbs instead of bread, but will be moister. Game hens may be done the same way, only 5 minutes on high checking and probably about 10-12 minutes per bird. You may want to use soy sauce for browning and color.

MOSTACCIOLI

1 large onion (diced)   2 T. sweet basil
4 cloves garlic (diced)   Salt and pepper
½ C. dry parsley flakes   3 lbs. ground beef
3 (No. 3) cans whole tomatoes   16-oz. noodles
2 small cans tomato paste   Parmesan cheese
¾ C. sugar

Put some bacon grease in large pan and brown the 1 large onion, diced; 4 cloves garlic, diced; and ½ C. dry parsley flakes until onions turn yellow. Add 3 No. 3 cans whole tomatoes. Add 2 small cans tomato paste plus 2 cans water. Add ¾ C. sugar and 2 T. sweet basil and salt and pepper to taste. Simmer slowly; add water to avoid sticking. While this is simmering, brown 3 lbs. ground beef. Mix ground beef with all of the above. Add tomato juice, if too thick. Cook slowly for 1 hour, stirring often. Cook 16-oz. pkg. noodles by directions on package, drain. Let sauce simmer a lengthy amount of time. In pan put a thin layer of sauce, then parmesan cheese, then noodles, cheese and meat. Repeat ending with sauce. Bake for 30 minutes at 350°.

PAN PIZZA

1 C. flour
2 eggs
⅔ C. milk

Salt
Pepper

Mix the above ingredients together and pour into a greased pan. Top with spaghetti or tomato sauce, herbs, cheese and meat of your choice. Bake at 425° for 25-30 minutes.

CALICO BEANS

½ lb. hamburger
½ lb. bacon
1 medium onion (chopped)
½ C. catsup
½ C. white sugar
⅔ C. brown sugar
2 T. vinegar

1 tsp. dry mustard
1 tsp. salt
1 (202) can of each:
lima beans
pork and beans
kidney beans (drained)
butter beans

Brown and drain the hamburger and bacon and add onion. Add all of the other ingredients and mix well. Bake in casserole at 350° for about 1 hour.

SPAGHETTI AND MEAT

2 T. shortening	2 C. tomato juice
1 lb. ground beef	1 C. catsup
1 small onion (finely chopped)	1 tsp. salt
1 C. broken, uncooked spaghetti	¼ tsp. pepper

Melt the shortening in skillet; add meat and onions; brown on medium heat until meat loses its red color. Place spaghetti over meat and onions. Add remaining ingredients; stir just enough to blend. Place cover on skillet. When steam escapes freely turn to simmer and cook 45 minutes.

CABBAGE MEAT CASSEROLE

1-1½ lb. hamburger	½ C. water
¼ C. onion	Grated cheese
½ C. uncooked Minute Rice	Raw cabbage
1 can tomato soup	

Grease 9x13-inch baking dish. Line bottom with raw cabbage. Brown the hamburger with onion. Add ½ C. uncooked rice. Stir in salt and pepper to taste. Put on cabbage. Pour over the tomato soup and water. Place grated cheese on top. Cover tight. Bake 350° for 1 hour.

SALISBURY STEAK

1 can cream of mushroom soup
1½ lbs. ground beef
½ C. dry bread crumbs

¼ C. finely chopped onion
1 egg (slightly beaten)
⅓ C. water

Mix ¼ C. of the soup, the ground beef, bread crumbs, onion and egg. Shape into 6 patties. Brown patties in skillet, pour off fat. Add remaining soup and water. Cover and cook over low heat 20 minutes or until done, stirring occasionally.

BEEF KOW

1 lb. round steak (sliced in
 thin strips)
1 T. soy sauce
1 slice ginger root (chopped)
1 clove garlic (minced)
2 T. oil
1 C. snow peas
½ C. mushrooms (sliced)

3 stalks Chinese cabbage
1 med. onion (sliced)
1 can bamboo shoots (sliced)
1 can water chestnuts (sliced)
1¼ C. chicken broth
2 T. cornstarch
2 T. soy sauce
2 tsp. oyster sauce

Marinate 1 hour the steak, soy sauce, ginger root and garlic. In wok cook beef in the oil; set aside. Stir-fry the peas, mushrooms, cabbage, onion, bamboo and water chestnuts in the beef juices. Return the beef to wok. Mix the chicken broth, cornstarch, soy sauce, and oyster sauce and add it to the wok and cook until thickened. Serve over rice and top with chow mein noodles.

CAKES

HEATH BAR CAKE

2 C. flour
1 C. brown sugar
½ C. white sugar

½ C. butter
¼ tsp. salt

Mix these 5 ingredients and take out ½ C. and set aside.

1 C. buttermilk
1 tsp. soda

1 egg
1 tsp. vanilla

Mix these 4 ingredients and add to above mixture.

6 Heath Bars (crushed)

Mix as instructed above and put in 9x13-inch greased and floured pan. Put the ½ C. crumb mixture on top. Sprinkle 6 crushed Heath bars on top. Bake 30-35 minutes at 350°.

MILKY WONDER CAKE

6 Milky Way bars
  (or 13 Fun-Size bars)
1 C. butter or margarine
2 C. sugar
4 eggs

2½ C. sifted all-purpose flour
½ tsp. baking soda
1¼ C. buttermilk
1 tsp. vanilla
1 C. chopped nuts

Melt bars and ½ C. butter in saucepan over very low heat or in microwave. Beat remaining ½ C. butter and sugar until fluffy. Add eggs, 1 at a time; beat well. Add flour and baking soda, alternately with buttermilk; stir until smooth. Add melted candy, mixing well. Stir in vanilla and nuts. Bake in moderate oven (350°) 1 hour and 20 minutes or until top springs back when lightly touched. (Top will be quite dark.) Bake in bundt style pan. Cool in pan on wire rack 10 minutes. Remove from pan; cool completely. Frost if you wish.

"LOVE CAKE"

1 yellow cake mix
1 (16-oz.) can crushed pineapple
1 pkg. (large) vanilla pudding mix

1 large container Cool Whip
Coconut
Nuts

Mix and bake cake mix according to directions on box. After it cools, punch holes in it and pour the can of crushed pineapple over it, juice and all. While cake is cooling, make the pudding mix and let it cool and then spread it on top of the pineapple. Then spread on the Cool Whip and add a layer of coconut and a layer of nuts. Refrigerate. This you will LOVE.

ITALIAN COCONUT CREME CAKE

2 C. sugar
½ C. oil
1 stick margarine
6 egg yolks (save the whites)
2 C. sifted flour

1 tsp. baking soda
1 C. buttermilk
1 tsp. vanilla
⅔ C. nuts
1 C. coconut

Cream together the sugar, oil, margarine and egg yolks. Add flour, baking soda, buttermilk, vanilla, nuts and coconut. Beat egg whites until stiff and fold into cake batter. Bake in 350° oven.

For Frosting: 8-oz. cream cheese, softened; ½ stick margarine, softened; and 1 box of powdered sugar and vanilla. You can make ½ of this recipe and it will fit in a 9x9-inch pan.

RAINBOW CAKE

2 ¼ C. cake flour
½ tsp. baking soda
3 tsp. baking powder
½ C. shortening

1 C. sugar
1 pkg. Jell-o, any flavor
3 eggs (beaten)
1 C. milk

Sift flour, soda, and baking powder three times. Cream the shortening, add sugar, Jell-o and cream together. Add eggs, 1 at a time, and beat well. Add milk to mixture a little at a time and beat well. Put in two greased layer pans and bake at 375° for 25-30 minutes.

PEANUT BUTTER CUPCAKES

½ C. brown sugar
½ C. sifted flour
2 T. margarine (melted)
¼ C. peanut butter
½ tsp. cinnamon
½ C. peanut butter
⅓ C shortening

1 ½ C. brown sugar
2 eggs
2 C. sifted flour
½ tsp. salt
½ tsp. cinnamon
1 C. milk
2 tsp. baking powder

Combine first 5 ingredients until crumbly; set aside. Cream peanut butter and shortening. Slowly beat in brown sugar. Add eggs, 1 at a time, beating until fluffy. Sift together flour, salt, cinnamon and baking powder; add alternately with milk, beating after each addition. Fill paper bake cups in muffin pans ½ full. Top with crumbly mixture. Bake at 375° for 18-20 minutes. Makes 30 cupcakes.

QUICK FUDGE FROSTING

1 C. sugar
¼ C. cocoa
¼ C. margarine
½ C. milk

2 T. white syrup
1/8 tsp. salt
1½-2 C. sifted powdered sugar
1 tsp. vanilla

Mix in saucepan sugar and cocoa. Add butter and milk, syrup and salt. Stir and bring to full rolling boil. Boil and cook 3 minutes or more stirring occasionally. Must be thick and coat spoon. Cool and beat in powdered sugar and flavoring.

PECAN CANDY CAKE

½ lb. (1⅓ C.) candied red cherries
(cut in quarters)
½ lb. (1 C.) candied pineapple
(coarsely chopped)
½ lb. (1½ C.) pitted dates
(coarsely snipped)

1 T. flour
4⅓ C. coarsely chopped pecans
(1 lb. shelled)
4-oz. (1¼ C.) flaked coconut
1 can (14-oz.) Eagle Brand milk

Preheat oven to 250°. Grease and flour a 9x3-inch tube pan with removable bottom. Combine the cherries, pineapple, and dates in very large bowl. Sprinkle with flour. Toss to coat well. Add pecans and coconut; toss to mix. Add milk, stir to mix well. Spoon into pan smoothing top. Bake at 250° for 1½ hours. Makes 1 9-inch cake, round spring form pan. Cool in pan on rack. Remove. Wrap tightly in foil. Refrigerate at least 2 weeks. Cake cuts best when cold. Slice very thin with serrated knife. Make at least 2 weeks ahead so flavors can mellow. Yield: 32 thin slices at 218 calories per slice.

QUICK AND EASY FROSTING

1 (15-oz.) can crushed pineapple   3½-oz. pkg. instant vanilla
                                     pudding

When a quick and easy frosting or topping is needed for a cake, add 1 (15-oz.) can crushed pineapple (juice and all) to a small pkg. (3½-oz.) of instant vanilla pudding. Stir until well mixed and ready to spread.

TURTLE CAKE

1 chocolate cake mix   1 C. chocolate chips
1 pkg. (12-oz.) caramels   ½ C. evaporated milk
1 C. nutmeats   ¾ C. butter

Bake ½ cake mix. Melt butter and add canned milk, poured over the baked ½ of the cake. On the other ½ cake mix put chocolate chips and nut meats and bake.

LEMON PINEAPPLE RIBBON CAKE

1 pkg. lemon cake mix	3 eggs
¾ C. water	8¼-oz. can crushed pineapple
⅓ C. oil	(drained, but reserve liquid)

FILLING:

¼ C. sugar	2 T. margarine (softened)
1 T. cornstarch	2 T. pineapple liquid
8-oz. cream cheese	1 egg

Heat oven to 350°. In a large bowl blend all cake ingredients, except for the pineapple, at low speed and then 2 minutes at high speed. Fold in the pineapple. Pour ⅔ of batter into prepared pan. Beat filling ingredients at high speed until smooth and creamy. Pour filling over batter in pan and spread to cover. Pour rest of batter over filling mixture and bake for 45-55 minutes. Frost cooled cake with your favorite lemon frosting.

7-UP CAKE

1 pkg. yellow cake mix	1 (12-oz.) bottle 7-Up
1 pkg. French vanilla instant pudding	½ C. walnuts (chopped)
¾ C. oil	½ C. shredded coconut
3 eggs	

TOPPING:

2 envelopes Dream Whip	1 pkg. French vanilla
1½ C. cold milk	instant pudding

Prepare cake from first 5 ingredients. Bake in an oiled and floured 9x12-inch pan for 45 minutes. When cool, frost.

For Topping: Beat Dream Whip and cold milk until very stiff, then add French vanilla instant pudding and beat well. Spread on cake. Sprinkle with the chopped walnuts and coconut.

ORANGE-PINEAPPLE CAKE

1 yellow cake mix
3 eggs

¾ C. oil
1 can mandarin oranges
(include juice)

FROSTING:
No. 2 can crushed pineapple
1 box vanilla instant pudding

1 tsp. vanilla
9-oz. Cool Whip

Beat cake mix, eggs, and oil together. Then add mandarin oranges with juice. Beat with mixer. Bake in 2 greased or wax-lined 8-inch or 9-inch pans. Bake at 350° for 25-30 minutes.

For Frosting: Mix pineapple, instant pudding, vanilla. Fold in Cool Whip. Frost and fill between layers. Keep refrigerated.

ITALIAN CREME CAKE

1 C. buttermilk
1 tsp. soda
½ C. margarine
½ C. shortening
2 C. sugar
5 egg yolks

2 C. flour
1 tsp. vanilla
5 egg whites
1 C. chopped pecans
1 (3½-oz.) can flake coconut

FROSTING:
1 (8-oz.) softened cream cheese
½ C. butter

1 tsp. vanilla
1 lb. powdered sugar

Combine buttermilk and soda. Cream margarine, shortening and sugar with buttermilk and soda. Add 5 egg yolks and beat well. Add dry ingredients with buttermilk alternately. Add vanilla. Beat 5 egg whites until stiff and fold into batter. Add pecans and coconut. Bake in 3 9-inch floured pans at 350° for 40-45 minutes. Frost with above frosting.

CREME DE MENTHE CAKE WITH SPREAD

1 white cake recipe   3 T. green creme de menthe

Mix favorite white cake according to directions, adding 3 T. creme de menthe and bake in well greased 9x13-inch pan. Cool.

SPREAD:
1 can (16-oz.) fudge topping   3 T. creme de menthe
1 container (9-oz.) whipped topping

Spread cake with fudge topping (you will not use the entire can). Then top with whipped topping mixed with 3 T. creme de menthe. Refrigerate.

FRUIT COCKTAIL CAKE

1 C. sugar   ½ tsp. salt
1½ C. flour   1 tsp. soda
1 can (16-oz.) fruit cocktail   ½ tsp. vanilla
  with syrup   1 egg

TOPPING:
1 C. brown sugar   ½ C. chopped nuts

Mix dry ingredients in a bowl; add egg, vanilla and fruit cocktail. Pour into an 8x10-inch pan. Sprinkle 1 C. brown sugar over all; then sprinkle with ½ C. nuts. Bake in 325° oven for 40 minutes. Serve with whipped cream.

CHOCOLATE SHEET CAKE

1 ¼ C. margarine or butter
½ C. unsweetened cocoa
1 C. water
2 C. unsifted flour
1 ½ C. firmly packed brown sugar
1 tsp. baking soda
1 tsp. ground cinnamon

½ tsp. salt
1 (14-oz.) can Eagle Brand
    sweetened condensed milk
2 eggs
1 tsp. vanilla extract
1 C. confectioner's sugar
1 C. chopped nuts

Preheat oven to 350°. In small saucepan, melt 1 C. margarine, stir in ¼ C. cocoa, then water. Bring to a boil; remove from heat. In large mixer bowl, combine flour, brown sugar, baking soda, cinnamon and salt. Add cocoa mixture; beat well. Stir in ⅓ C. Eagle Brand, eggs, and vanilla. Pour into greased 15x10-inch jelly roll pan. Bake 15 minutes or until cake springs back when lightly touched. In small saucepan, melt remaining ¼ C.margarine; stir in remaining ¼ C. cocoa and Eagle Brand. Stir in confectioner's sugar and nuts. Spread on warm cake.

COCOA CHIFFON CAKE

½ C. baking cocoa
¾ C. boiling water
8 eggs (separated)
½ tsp. cream of tartar
1 ¾ C. sifted cake flour

1 ¾ C. sugar
1 ½ tsp. baking soda
1 tsp. salt
½ C. salad oil
2 tsp. vanilla

Mix cocoa with boiling water and set aside. Beat egg whites with cream of tartar until very stiff peaks form. Sift together dry ingredients into a mixing bowl, make a well in the center and add oil, egg yolks, cocoa mixture and vanilla; beat well. Fold in egg whites. Pour into an ungreased 10-inch tube pan. Cut through batter with spatula. Bake at 325° for 55 minutes. Increase temperature to 350° and bake 10 minutes longer or until done. Invert to cool. Frost with your favorite chocolate frosting.

DESSERTS

GRAHAM CRACKER TORTE DESSERT

1 can lemon pie filling	1 C. milk
1 C. sugar	¾ C. coconut
½ C. margarine	2¼ C. graham cracker crumbs
2 eggs (separated)	2 tsp. baking powder
1½-oz. pkg. whipped topping	

Cream sugar and margarine. Beat egg yolks. Add yolks, milk and ½ C. coconut to creamed mixture. Blend in crumbs and baking powder. Pour into 2 8-9-inch square pans that are greased and floured. Bake 350° for 25-30 minutes. Cool. Put layers together with ½ can filling. Frost with mixture of prepared topping and remaining lemon filling. Sprinkle with rest of coconut that has been toasted. Refrigerate.

DATE PUDDING

1 C. dates (chopped)	1 T. butter or margarine
1 tsp. soda	1 egg
1 C. hot water	1⅓ C. flour
1 C. sugar	½ C. nutmeats

Put soda and hot water over dates and let cool. Add rest of ingredients and mix together. Bake in 9-inch square pan which has been greased. Bake in a 350° oven. Serve with whipped cream or Cool Whip.

CHOCOLATE MOUSSE

1 tsp. unflavored gelatin
1 T. cold water
2 T. boiling water
½ C. sugar

¼ C. cocoa
1 tsp. vanilla
1 C. whipping cream (very cold)

In a small bowl sprinkle gelatin over cold water. Stir; let stand 1 minute to soften; add boiling water. Stir until gelatin is completely dissolved (mixture must be clear). Stir together sugar and cocoa in small cold mixing bowl. Add cream and vanilla. Beat at medium speed until stiff peaks form. Pour in gelatin mixture and beat until well blended. Spoon into serving dishes. Chill ½ hour. Makes 4 ½ C. servings.

CHERRY MASH

2 C. sugar
¾ C. Carnation milk
Dash salt
12 large marshmallows

¼ C. margarine
1 tsp. vanilla
1 (12-oz.) pkg. cherry chips
    (I don't use whole pkg.)

SECOND LAYER:
1 (6-oz.) pkg. chocolate chips
¼ C. margarine

¾ C. peanut butter
½ C. crushed salted peanuts

Combine first 5 ingredients in pan over medium heat. Boil 5 minutes and remove from heat. Add cherry chips and vanilla. Pour into 9x13-inch buttered pan. Melt chocolate chips. Add margarine, peanut butter and peanuts. Spread over cherry mixture and chill. Cut into squares.

132

CHEESE CUPS

1 box Vanilla Wafers	2 tsp. lemon juice
2 (8-oz.) pkg. cream cheese	1 tsp. vanilla
¾ C. sugar	1 can pie filling (any flavor)
2 eggs	

Beat cream cheese until fluffy. Add sugar, eggs, lemon juice, add vanilla and beat together until mixture is smooth. Put a vanilla wafer in a tart cup. Fill ¾ full with cream cheese mixture and bake at 350° for 15 minutes. Let cool and top with desired pie filling. These freeze well.

CHERRY PIZZA

CRUST:

1 large cream cheese	1 tsp. vanilla
2 eggs	⅓ C. pecans
½ C. sugar	

Spread in pizza pan and bake 15 minutes at 350°.

TOPPING:

1 pkg. (20-oz.) frozen cherries	3 T. cornstarch
⅔ C. sugar	

Cook over moderate heat until thickened. Take off stove and add 1 T. butter, ½ tsp. almond flavor. Cool, pour over crust and bake 15 minutes. Can be used with any fresh fruit.

CHERRY DELIGHT

40 large marshmallows
1 C. milk
1 carton whipped topping
1⅓ C. graham cracker crumbs

⅓ C. melted margarine
3 T. sugar
1 can cherry pie filling

Dissolve 40 large marshmallows in 1 C. milk in double boiler. Cool. Add 1 carton whipped topping. Crush enough graham crackers to make 1⅓ C. Add ⅓ C. melted margarine and 3 T. sugar and mix good. Put in 9x13-inch pan; save some to spread on top. Pour ½ of marshmallow mixture over crumbs. Let set then spoon 1 can cherry pie filling over this. Top with rest of marshmallow mix; then sprinkle rest of crumbs over top.

BREAD PUDDING

3 slices dry bread
½ C. raisins
¾ C. sugar
1 T. flour

2 C. milk
2 eggs
½ tsp. vanilla
Nutmeg to taste

Break bread into pieces. Put ½ in bottom of buttered baking dish. Add raisins and rest of the bread. Beat eggs, add sugar, flour and milk; mix well. Pour over bread, let stand 1 hour and then bake at 350° for 45 minutes. Serve with a sauce if desired.

BANANA SPLIT DESSERT

2 C. graham cracker crumbs
2 C. powdered sugar
4 bananas (sliced)
1½ C. margarine
12-oz. carton whipped topping

2 eggs
Maraschino cherries
20-oz. crushed, drained, pineapple
1½ C. chopped pecans

For Crust: Mix graham crackers and ½ C. melted margarine; press into 9x13-inch pan and chill.

For Filling: Beat together 1 C. margarine, powdered sugar and eggs. Beat with mixer at least 15 minutes. Pour onto crust.

For Topping: Top with the sliced bananas, crushed pineapple, chopped pecans, cherry pieces, and whipped topping. Serves 10 easy. (Patti only puts ½ C. chopped pecans in hers.)

APPLE CRISP

4-5 C. sliced apples
⅓ C. water
½ C. sugar
1 tsp. cinnamon
1 C. flour
1 C. sugar

1 tsp. baking powder
½ tsp. cinnamon
½ tsp. salt
1 egg
½ C. oil

Place apples in 9x13-inch pan. Sprinkle over them the water. Mix ½ C. sugar and 1 tsp. cinnamon and sprinkle over apples. Sift together flour, sugar, baking powder, cinnamon and salt. Beat egg and oil together and add to flour mixture. Spoon and spread over apples. Bake 350° for 35 minutes or until apples are tender and crust lightly brown.

ANGEL DELIGHT

2 envelopes minute gelatin	½ C. cold water
½ C. sugar	1 C. marshmallow creme
1 tsp. vanilla	1½ C. whipping cream
2 egg whites (beaten stiff)	Dash of salt
1 C. crushed pineapple (drained)	Angel food cake

Dissolve gelatin and sugar in cold water and pineapple juice. Cool until partially set. Beat until light and fluffy. Then add beaten egg whites, marshmallow creme and stiffly whipped cream, vanilla and salt. Stir in pineapple. Pour over angel food cake lined in pan bottom and chill. Keep refrigerated!

APPLE CRINKLES

4 C. sliced apples	2 T. flour
1 C. sugar	

TOPPING:

½ C. brown sugar	½ C. softened margarine
½ C. oatmeal	Dash of salt
½ C. flour	

Mix apples, flour and sugar and place in baking dish. Mix the rest of the ingredients together and spread over apples. Bake at 350° until done. Can also use other fruit in place of apples.

PEACH DESSERT

1 large can peaches
1 pkg. yellow cake mix

1 C. brown sugar
1 stick margarine (melted)

Place peaches in large Pyrex dish (may cut peaches if desired). Put dry cake mix on top of peaches. Sprinkle brown sugar on top of cake mix. Pour melted margarine evenly on top of brown sugar. Bake at 325° for 50-60 minutes or until brown.

CHERRY DESSERT

16 graham crackers
¼ C. margarine

½ C. powdered sugar
2 cans cherry pie filling

FILLING:
2 eggs
½ C. sugar

1 large cream cheese

Make graham cracker crust from the first 3 ingredients and pat into 9x13-inch pan. Blend the filling ingredients together until smooth and pour on top of crust. Bake at 350° for 20 minutes. Cool. Put the cherry pie filling on top of this and frost with Cool Whip or Dream Whip.

CHOCOLATE MOUSSE

4 C. milk	1½ lbs. Hershey's semi-sweet
1 C. sugar	baking chocolate
3 egg yolks	1½ pt. heavy cream (whipped)
1½-oz. cornstarch	

Melt chocolate in double boiler over hot water. Mix sugar in saucepan with most of milk; place over low flame and bring to boil. Separately beat egg yolks with the balance of the milk, gradually adding the cornstarch. Combine this mixture with the boiling milk and sugar. Continue to cook over low flame, stirring constantly, until mixture reaches the consistency of custard. Add melted chocolate. Remove from heat and let cool. When mixture is thoroughly cool, fold in whipped cream. Spoon into cups or parfait glasses and chill. Makes 12 servings. (It is delicious.)

FRUIT BARS

½ C. margarine	5 eggs
2 C. sugar	1 tsp. vanilla
3 C. flour	1 tsp. almond
1 can fruit pie filling	Cinnamon and sugar

Cream together the margarine, sugar and flour. Add the eggs, 1 at a time, then the vanilla and almond. Beat well. Spread ½ this batter on a greased sheet pan. Spread on pie filling. Top with remaining batter. Sprinkle with sugar and/or cinnamon. Bake 25 minutes at 350°F.

138

GRAHAM DATE LOAF

1 lb. graham crackers
1 lb. diced marshmallows
1 C. whipped cream

1 lb. pitted dates
1 C. nuts

Roll graham crackers fine. Combine with remaining ingredients. Mix thoroughly. Form into a roll and wrap in waxed paper. Let stand a time before serving. Slice and garnish with whipped cream.

PINK DESSERT

1 large cottage cheese (drained)
1½ pkg. strawberry Jell-o (dry)
1 large can fruit cocktail (drained)
1 carton Cool Whip

1 small can crushed pineapple
  (drained)
2 C. small marshmallows

Mix all together with cottage cheese and Jell-o. Add the Cool Whip, mix well. Let stand overnight in refrigerator.

COUNTRY ICE CREAM

9 eggs
5 C. sugar
5 tsp. vanilla
2 tsp. lemon extract

1 ½ tsp. salt
2 cartons whipping cream
2 cartons Half and Half
Milk

Beat the eggs, gradually add the sugar, vanilla and lemon extract. Beat whipping cream until stiff, add this and the salt. Fold in the Half and Half. Put in a gallon and a half freezer; add milk to mixture until 1-inch from the top. Stir well. Ready to freeze.

COUNTRY STYLE VANILLA ICE CREAM

4 eggs
2 ½ C. sugar
5 C. (approx.) milk

4 C. whipping cream
2 T. vanilla
¼ tsp. salt

In a large mixing bowl beat eggs until foamy. Gradually add sugar; beat until thickened. Add cream, vanilla and salt and mix thoroughly. Pour into can; add milk and stir well. Freeze. Makes 4 qts.

ANGEL FOOD SNOWBALLS

2 loaf angel foods (10-oz. size)   Juice of 2 oranges
2 lbs. powdered sugar   ⅓ C. butter or margarine (melted)

Cut angel food cake into 1¼x1½-inch size cubes. Crust may be removed before cutting if a more perfect product is desired (more wasteful, however). Add juice and melted butter to sifted powdered sugar (icing should not be too stiff). Green or pink or yellow food coloring may be added to make a delicate tint. Ice all sides of angel food square and cover with coconut. Cream may be substituted for margarine if a harder icing is desired.

APPLE CRISP

Slice apples in buttered 9x13-inch pan. Sprinkle with cinnamon and dash of salt. Add ½ C. water.

TOPPING:
1½ C. flour   ⅔ C. butter
2 C. sugar

Mix together and cut in butter. Bake at 350° for 40 minutes.

APPLE ROLLS

2 C. flour	3 T. oil
2 T. sugar	¼ C. margarine
1 tsp. salt	½ C. milk
2 tsp. baking powder	1 egg
Apple slices	½ C. sugar and ½ tsp. cinnamon
Additional margarine	2 C. water
2 C. brown sugar	Additional cinnamon

Sift dry ingredients. Cut in margarine and oil. Add milk and egg. Stir until flour is moistened. Roll out ½-inch thick in a rectangle. Slice 5 apples or use frozen apple slices that are thawed and drained. Sprinkle slices with sugar and cinnamon and spread over dough. Dot with 3 T. margarine. Roll up as cinnamon roll and slice ½-inch thick. Place in greased 9x13-inch pan. Combine brown sugar, water, and ¼ tsp. cinnamon. Bring to boil. Pour over rolls and bake in 350° oven 35-40 minutes. Serve warm with cream or ice cream.

COUNTRY APPLE DESSERT

1 pkg. Pillsbury Plus yellow cake mix	½ C. chopped walnuts
⅓ C. margarine or butter (softened)	1 tsp. cinnamon
1 egg	1 egg
20-oz. can apple fruit pie filling	1 tsp. vanilla
½ C. brown sugar (packed)	1 C. dairy sour cream

Heat oven to 350°. In large bowl combine cake mix, margarine, 1 egg at low speed until crumbly. Press in ungreased 9x13-inch pan. Spread with pie filling. Combine brown sugar, nuts and cinnamon; sprinkle over apples. In small bowl blend sour cream, egg and vanilla. Pour over sugar mixture. Bake at 350° for 30-40 minutes or until sides are golden. Serve warm or cool. Refrigerate any leftovers.

BING CHERRY JELLO

1 can cherry pie filling
¾ C. sugar
1 (3-oz.) pkg. cherry Jell-o

1 can Coke or cola
1 can crushed pineapple
¾ C. nuts

Bring the pie filling and sugar to a boil and add the remaining ingredients. Chill.

SPICED APPLE SUNDAES

1 (15-16-oz.) jar chunky applesauce
  or homemade applesauce
2 T. maple syrup
½ tsp. cinnamon
½ tsp. vanilla

¼ tsp. salt
¼ tsp. allspice
1/8 tsp. ginger
1 pt. vanilla ice cream
¼ C. pecans or walnuts

Heat applesauce and spices in pan for 10 minutes, uncovered. Scoop ice cream in bowls and top with applesauce mixture and sprinkle with nuts.

BROWNIE PUDDING

1 C. flour	2 tsp. baking powder
½ tsp. salt	¾ C. sugar
2 T. cocoa	½ C. milk
1 tsp. vanilla	2 T. margarine
1 C. nuts	

Mix all together and pour into a 9-inch pan.

TOPPING:

¾ C. brown sugar	¼ C. cocoa
1¾ C. hot water	

Mix together and pour over batter. Bake 350° for 40 minutes. Serve with whipped cream or ice cream.

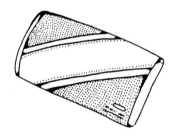

LEMON CHEESE CAKE

1 (8-oz.) pkg. cream cheese	1 pkg. lemon instant pudding mix
2 C. milk	8-inch graham cracker crust

Stir cream cheese until smooth, blend in ½ C. milk, add rest of milk and pudding mix. Beat slowly 1 minute. Pour into crust. Top with Cool Whip and sprinkle with graham cracker crumbs. Chill.

CHERRY FLUFF

21-oz. cherry pie filling
8-oz. container Cool Whip
14-oz. can sweetened condensed milk

8-oz. can crushed pineapple
1 C. nuts

Fold all ingredients together. Pour into glass serving bowl; chill.

CHOCOLATE FROZEN ANGEL DESSERT

1 small pkg. chocolate chips
2 T. sugar
3 T. cold water

3 eggs (separated)
1 C. whipped cream
1 tsp. vanilla
Angel food cake

Melt chocolate in double boiler. Stir in sugar and water, remove from heat. Stir in egg yolks. Beat smooth with spoon. Beat egg whites stiff and fold into chocolate mixture. Fold in whipped cream and vanilla. Tear pieces of angel food cake and cover bottom of pan. Pour half of chocolate mixture over cake. Top with another layer of cake and pour over the rest of the chocolate mixture. Freeze.

DATE ROLL

2 C. sugar
¼ C. butter
1 C. nuts

1 C. milk
1 lb. dates

Cook sugar, milk and butter over slow fire until mixture forms soft ball when tested in cold water. Remove from fire, add dates (stoned and cut into small pieces). Stir well, then add chopped nuts. Beat until stiff. Wet a bread paper and spread mixture on it. Let stand until cold, then roll.

CRANBERRY MOUSSE

1 pkg. (3-oz.) raspberry Jell-o
1 C. cranberry juice cocktail
   or water

1 can (16-oz.) Ocean Spray Cran-
   Raspberry sauce
2 C. whipped topping

In a saucepan heat juice cocktail to boiling; remove from heat, stir in Jell-o until dissolved. In a bowl, beat cran-raspberry sauce with mixer on high 1 minute. Stir in gelatin mixture. Chill in refrigerator 2½ hours or until thickened but not set. Fold in whipped topping until mixture is thoroughly blended. Spoon into dessert dishes or 9-inch prepared pie shells. Chill until firm.

FRUIT COCKTAIL DESSERT

COMBINE THESE:
1 ½ C. flour	1 tsp. soda
¾ C. sugar	¼ tsp. salt

To the above mixture, add 1 beaten egg and 1 large can of fruit cocktail. Pour in pan and on top sprinkle ½ C. nut meats and ½ C. brown sugar. Bake in 9x12-inch pan in moderate oven (350°) for 25-30 minutes. Top with whipped cream.

MAGIC MARSHMALLOW CRESCENT PUFFS

¼ C. sugar	16 marshmallows
1 tsp. cinnamon	¼ C. melted butter or margarine
2 cans crescent dinner rolls	¼ C. chopped dates

ICING:
½ C. sifted powdered sugar	½ tsp. vanilla
2-3 T. milk	

Combine sugar and cinnamon. Separate crescent dough into 16 triangles. Dip marshmallow in butter, then sugar-cinnamon mixture. Wrap a dough triangle around each marshmallow completely covering marshmallow and squeezing edges of dough tightly to seal. Dip sealed side in butter and place buttered side down in greased muffin tins. Place tins on cookie sheet during baking. Bake at 375° for 10-15 minutes or until golden brown. Immediately remove from pan and drizzle with icing. Sprinkle with nuts. Serve warm. Makes 16 puffs.

MALLOW MELLOW

Delight your sweet tooth when chill winds blow.

2 C. miniature marshmallows
2 T. butter
½ C. creamy peanut butter
1 C. coarsely chopped pecans

1 pkg. (12-oz.) semi-sweet
  chocolate bits
½ tsp. vanilla

Line an 8x8-inch pan with aluminum foil. Place marshmallows in bottom of pan. Melt butter in saucepan over medium heat. Stir in peanut butter and chocolate bits. Stir until chocolate has melted. Remove from heat and add vanilla, blending thoroughly. Fold in pecans. Spoon over marshmallows in pan. Cover securely with foil. Refrigerate until thoroughly cooled, at least 1 hour. Remove foil and cut into pieces.

PEPPERMINT DESSERT

30 dark chocolate Oreo cookies
1 jar marshmallow creme
½ stick butter
2 envelopes Dream Whip
  (prepare as directed)

5 drops peppermint flavoring
3-oz. cream cheese (optional)
Red or green food coloring
  (if desired)

Crush the cookies. Mix with the butter or margarine. Mix together rest of ingredients and fold onto the cookies.

PINEAPPLE AND LEMON JELL-O DESSERT

16 graham crackers (crushed
½ C. butter
4 egg yolks
1 C. sugar

1 C. crushed pineapple
½ pkg. lemon Jell-o
4 egg whites
½ C. sugar

Mix the graham crackers and butter like pie crust. Beat egg yolks then add sugar and pineapple. Mix and cook until syrupy. Add lemon Jell-o; let cool. Beat egg whites adding the ½ C. sugar. Fold into above mixture. Line a pan with ½ of graham cracker mixture, pour the above mixture over the graham cracker mixture then sprinkle the remaining crackers over this mixture.

PLUM PUDDING

1 C. sugar
½ tsp. cloves
1 C. ground or chopped suet
1 C. (scant) raisins
1 tsp. salt

1½ C. flour
1 tsp. cinnamon
1 C. sour milk
1 tsp. soda
1 tsp. nutmeg

Mix all together and put in a mold or a cloth which you wet first and tie with string. Leave a little room for it to raise. Put in a large kettle and cover with water. Boil for 3 hours; add more water after 1½ hours. Or cook ½ hour in a pressure cooker with steam spouting (don't put control on). Then put on control and cook 1 hour at 5 lbs. pressure. Use 6 C. water. Make a sauce from 2 C. water, 1 C. sugar, 2 T. cornstarch, ½ tsp. nutmeg or ½ tsp. cinnamon. Boil to thicken. The pudding can be frozen.

PUMPKIN SPICE DESSERT

1 C. Bisquick	½ tsp. salt
½ C. oats	1 tsp. cinnamon
½ C. brown sugar	½ tsp. ginger
¼ C. firm margarine	¼ tsp. cloves
16-oz. can pumpkin	½ C. chopped nuts
1 (3-oz.) can evaporated milk	½ C. brown sugar
2 eggs	2 T. firm margarine
¾ C. sugar	

SPICED WHIPPED CREAM:

1 C. whipping cream	1 tsp. grated orange peel
1 T. sugar	½ tsp. cinnamon

Combine Bisquick, oats, brown sugar, and margarine until crumbly. Press in 9x13-inch pan; bake 10 minutes. Cool slightly. Beat pumpkin, milk, eggs, sugar, salt and spices. Pour over baked layer. Bake 20 minutes. Mix nuts, brown sugar and margarine until crumbly. Sprinkle on filling. Bake until set (15-20 minutes). Cool completely. Beat whipping cream until soft peaks form. Beat in sugar, orange peel, and cinnamon. Serve this topping with dessert.

RICE PUDDING

¾ C. uncooked rice	2 tsp. grated orange peel
2 large eggs (lightly beaten)	½ tsp. vanilla
1½ C. milk	½ tsp. salt
1½ C. heavy cream	½ C. raisins
½ C. sugar	½ tsp. cinnamon
2 tsp. grated lemon peel	Whipped cream

Prepare rice in 1½ C. water according to package directions. Meanwhile heat oven to 350°. Grease 8-inch square baking dish. In large bowl combine eggs, cream, sugar, lemon and orange peels, vanilla and salt. Beat until well blended. Stir in raisins. Put cooked rice in greased baking dish and then spoon mixture over the rice. Sprinkle with cinnamon. Put baking dish in pan of hot water and put into oven. Bake 45 minutes . Let set 3 hours or overnight. Serve with whipped cream.

BUTTER PECAN ICE CREAM

2 C. sugar
4 eggs
Dash of salt

2 pkgs. butter pecan
instant pudding mix
1 (9-oz.) Cool Whip
½ gal. whole milk

Beat eggs and sugar and salt. Add pudding mix and Cool Whip. Blend well and then add milk and stir. Makes 1 gal.

STRAWBERRY DESSERT

1 box frozen strawberries
2 sliced bananas
1 large can pineapple (drained)
1 large cream cheese (softened)

¾ C. sugar
½ C. pecans (optional)
1 large Cool Whip

In blender, mix together all ingredients except the Cool Whip. Fold in the Cool Whip. Pour into can pan and refrigerate until firm.

STRAWBERRY SALAD

2 (3-oz.) boxes strawberry Jell-o
2 (10-oz.) boxes frozen strawberries
2 C. boiling water

3 large bananas (mashed)
1 pt. sour cream

Dissolve gelatin in boiling water. Add strawberries, stirring occasionally, until thawed. Add bananas. Pour ½ mixture into 8x8-inch baking dish. Chill until firm. Spread sour cream on top of gelatin. Pour remaining mixture over sour cream.

RHUBARB PUDDING

3 C. diced rhubarb
¾ C. light brown sugar (firmly packed)
¼ tsp. nutmeg
¼ tsp. cinnamon
1 T. butter or margarine

½ C. sugar
1 egg (well beaten)
½ C. sifted all-purpose flour
¼ tsp. salt

Spread the diced rhubarb in a 1-qt. greased baking dish. Sprinkle with the brown sugar, nutmeg and cinnamon. Cream the butter and sugar, stir in the egg. Sift together the flour and salt. Add the flour to the egg and sugar mixture, stirring until smooth. Spread the batter over the fruit. Bake in a 350° oven for 45 minutes or until fruit is tender. May be served warm.

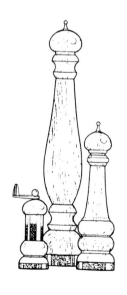

OLD FASHIONED CHRISTMAS PLUM PUDDING

½ C. dried currants	1 tsp. ground cinnamon
½ C. raisins	2 eggs
½ C. sugar	½ C. chopped walnuts
3 C. all purpose flour	¼ chopped citron (optional)
1 tsp. baking soda	¼ C. chopped orange peel
1 tsp. salt	1 apple (grated)
½ tsp. ginger	½ C. beef suet (chopped fine)
½ tsp. cloves	1½ C. whole milk
½ C. light molasses	Brandy

Soak currants and raisins overnight in ½ C. brandy or water. Sift together flour, baking soda, and spices. Thoroughly mix eggs and sugar. Add raisins and currants, nuts, citron, orange peel and apple. Stir in the suet, milk, and molasses and mix thoroughly. Wrap in a cloth and tie with string. Put in pan of boiling water and cook 3 hours. Serve with hard sauce. For Hard Sauce: 1 C. butter (melted), 2 C. powdered sugar, 1 tsp. vanilla.

PINEAPPLE BUTTERSCOTCH SQUARES

2 C. flour	2 eggs
¾ tsp. baking powder	1 C. drained crushed pineapple
¾ tsp. salt	⅓ C. nuts
⅓ C. shortening	6-oz. pkg. butterscotch chips
⅔ C. dark corn syrup	Powdered sugar
½ tsp. vanilla	

Sift flour, baking powder and salt. Set aside. Cream shortening. Add brown sugar. Beat in vanilla and eggs and stir in the pineapple. Mix dry ingredients, nuts and butterscotch chips. Bake in oiled 9x13-inch pan. Bake 350° for 25 minutes. Cool. Cut. Sprinkle with powdered sugar.

EASY FRUIT COBBLER

1 can (large size) sliced peaches
1 C. sugar
1 C. flour
2 tsp. baking powder

Pinch of salt
⅔ C. milk
1 tsp. vanilla

Empty peaches in 9x13-inch pan. Dot with butter and sprinkle with cinnamon or nutmeg. Top with a batter made from the remaining ingredients. Bake at 325° for 1 hour.

APRICOT DESSERT

8-oz. non dairy whipped topping
14-oz. can sweetened condensed milk

21-oz. can apricot pie filling
20-oz. can crushed pineapple
(undrained)

Combine all ingredients and whip with electric mixer until well blended. Pour into 9x13-inch pan and place in freezer. Serve frozen or remove from freezer a few minutes before serving time.

BANANA PUDDING CAKE

1 pkg. (4 serving size) banana cream
instant pudding
1 pkg. yellow cake mix
½ C. mashed bananas

4 eggs
1 C. water
¼ C. oil

Combine all ingredients in a bowl. Blend, then beat at medium speed for 2 minutes. Pour into greased and floured 10-inch tube pan. Bake at 350° for 50-55 minutes or until cake springs back when touched. Cool in pan for 15 minutes. Remove from pan and finish cooling on rack. Drizzle with 1 T. milk mixed with 1 C. sifted powdered sugar.

BREAD PUDDING

4 C. dry bread cubes	1 C. sugar
4 C. milk (scalded)	4 slightly beaten eggs
1 T. butter	1 tsp. vanilla
¼ tsp. salt	¾ C. raisins (opttional)

Mix bread with milk. Add butter, salt and sugar. Pour slowly over eggs; add vanilla and mix well. Pour into greased baking dish. Bake at 350° until firm, 50 minutes or so.

BREAD PUDDING

4 C. bread crumbs	2 egg yolks
4 C. milk or 1 tall can	¾ C. sugar
1 tsp. salt	1 tsp. vanilla
Dash of nutmeg	

If canned milk is used dilute with an equal amount of water. Soak bread crumbs in milk, add beaten eggs, salt and sugar. Pour into a greased pudding pan. Sprinkle the top sparingly with nutmeg. If you use vanilla, mix in with pudding mixture and leave off nutmeg. Bake in moderate oven about 30 minutes or until firm and brown. Beat the whites of eggs; spread on top and brown. Sometimes instead of putting meringue on top of pudding make a white sauce to pour over pudding when served. Make the sauce of milk, sugar and thickening, a lump of butter and a little vanilla.

CHERRY WHIP

1 can tapioca pudding
1 can cherry pie filling

1 container Cool Whip

Fold together, chill and serve.

CHOCOLATE ICE CREAM DESSERT

½ C. flour
¼ C. quick oatmeal
¼ C. brown sugar

½ gal. chocolate ice cream
1 small jar butterscotch topping
(2½-oz.)

Mix the flour, oatmeal, sugar and margarine and put in 9x13-inch pan, saving some for topping, and bake at 350° for 15 minutes. Soften the ice cream and spread on top of bottom layer. Pour butterscotch topping over the ice cream and top with remaining crumbs. Freeze.

BAKED CRANBERRY PUDDING

2 C. flour
1 C. sugar
2½ tsp. baking powder
½ lb. (2 C.) cranberries

3 T. shortening (melted)
⅔ C. milk
1 egg

Sift dry ingredients into mixing bowl. Add shortening, milk and egg; beat 2 minutes. Stir in cranberries. Bake in 9-inch square pan at 350° about 40 minutes. Serves 9. Serve with hot butter sauce.

For Hot Butter Sauce: Melt ¾ c. butter in double boiler. Add 1½ C. sugar and 1⅔ C. light cream. Mix well. Cook over hot water about 5 minutes. Stir occasionally. Serve hot.

QUICK COBBLER

2 cans cherry pie filling
1 box Jiffy cake mix (chocolate)

¼ C. margarine
½ C. pecans (chopped)

Spoon 1 can pie filling in 2-qt. casserole. Sprinkle ½ the cake mix over filling and dot with margarine; top with ½ of the pecans. Repeat each layer. Bake 35-40 minutes at 375°.

CREAMY RICE PUDDING

4 C. milk	1 C. Minute Rice
1 egg (well beaten)	1 pkg. Jell-o vanilla pudding mix

Gradually stir milk and egg into pudding mixture in a saucepan. Stir over medium heat until mixture comes to a boil. Remove from heat and pour into dessert dishes or bowl. Sprinkle with cinnamon. You may add raisins to this if you like.

FROSTY STRAWBERRY SQUARES

1 C. flour	¾ C. sugar
1 C. brown sugar	1 pkg. (10-oz.) frozen strawberries
½ C. nuts (chopped)	2 T. lemon juice
½ C. margarine (melted)	1 C. whipped cream or 1 pkg.
2 egg whites	(4½-oz.) Cool Whip

In a bowl stir together the flour, brown sugar, nuts and margarine. Spread into a 9x13-inch pan. Bake at 350° for 20 minutes, stirring occasionally. Cool. In a large mixer bowl combine eggs, sugar, berries and lemon juice. Beat at low speed until thick. Continue beating at high speed until stiff peaks form. Fold in Cool Whip. Sprinkle ⅔ crumb mixture into 9x13-inch pan. Spread on berry mixture and add remaining crumbs to top. Freeze at least 6 hours.

HEAVENLY ORANGE FLUFF

2 (3-oz.) pkgs. orange gelatin	2 cans mandarin oranges (drained)
2 C. boiling water	1 large can crushed pineapple
1 small can frozen orange juice	(not drained)
(undiluted)	

LEMON TOPPING:

1 (3-oz.) pkg. instant lemon pudding	1-1½ C. whipped topping
1 C. milk	

Dissolve gelatin in boiling water; add frozen orange juice. Add mandarin oranges and pineapple. Mix well. Pour into mold or 9x13x2-inch dish. When set, cover with lemon topping. To make topping add milk to instant pudding and beat with a beater until thickened. Fold in approximately 1-1½ C. whipped topping. Spread on to congealed gelatin.

CARAMEL DUMPLINGS

½ C. white sugar
2½ C. boiling water
1/8 tsp. salt
1 C. sugar
1 T. butter
½ C. white sugar

1½ C. flour
1/8 tsp. salt
1 T. baking powder
1 T. butter
½ C. milk
½ C. chipped nuts

Brown ½ C. white sugar in skillet. Add 2½ C. boiling water, 1/8 tsp. salt; add 1 C. sugar, 1 T. butter and boil 5 minutes. Pour in 9x13-inch pan. In bowl, mix ½ C. white sugar, 1½ C. flour, 1/8 tsp. salt, 1 T. baking powder, 1 T. butter, ½ C. milk, ½ C. chopped nuts. Drop by teaspoon in hot syrup. Bake at 350° until golden brown. Serve with pouring cream or whipped cream.

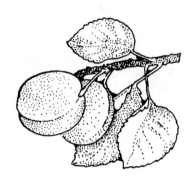

EASY PEACH COBBLER

½ C. butter or margarine
1 C. sugar
1 C. flour
1 tsp. baking powder

⅔ C. milk
1 qt. fresh or frozen peaches or
1 (32-oz.) can peaches (drained)

Melt butter. Combine sugar, flour, baking powder, and milk in mixing bowl; mix well. Pour melted butter over sugar mixture. Do not stir. Arrange peaches in 9x13-inch baking pan. Pour sugar mixture over top. Bake in preheated 325° oven for 30 minutes or until done.

APPLE COBBLER

7 C. peeled and sliced apples
¼ - ⅓ C. light brown sugar
2 T. all-purpose flour
½ tsp. cinnamon

¼ tsp. nutmeg
1/8 tsp. salt
2 T. lemon juice
2 T. butter or margarine

BISCUIT TOPPING:
1 C. flour
3 T. sugar
2 tsp. baking powder
⅓ C. powdered sugar

¼ tsp. salt
5 T. cold butter or margarine
⅓ C. milk

Preheat oven to 375°. Lightly grease an 8x8-inch baking dish. To make filling, combine apples, sugar, flour, cinnamon, nutmeg, salt and lemon juice in the prepared baking dish until well blended. Dot with the butter. To make topping, combine flour, sugar, baking powder and salt in a large bowl. With a pastry blender or two knives, cut in butter until mixture resembles coarse crumbs. Add milk, stirring with a fork, until dough just comes together. Dough will be sticky. Knead dough gently on a lightly floured surface 4-5 times, adding more flour, if necessary. Roll or pat dough into an 8-inch square. Place dough on apples and press down. Bake 40-45 minutes, or until golden and filling is bubbling. If biscuit browns too quickly, cover loosely with aluminum foil. Let cool at least 30 minutes before serving. Serve warm sprinkled with confectioner's sugar if you like.

APPLE CRISP

8 C. apples (sliced)
1½ C. brown sugar

1½ C. flour
1 C. butter or margarine

TOPPING:
2 C. oatmeal
1 tsp. salt

Cinnamon

If the apples are Jonathans or others with a tender skin, leave some of the skin on to make the dessert more colorful. Sprinkle the cinnamon over the slices. Mix the other ingredients and pour over the apples. Bake 40 minutes at 350° or until light brown and the apples are done.

BARS & COOKIES

ALMOND BARS

CRUST:

4 C. flour

1 T. sugar

1½ tsp. salt

1½ T. vinegar

1½ tsp. baking powder

1½ C. shortening

1 egg

1 C. water

FILLING:

4 T. almond extract

2 eggs

3 C. sugar

6 T. flour

½ C. milk

Mix crust ingredients together as you would a pie dough. Divide into 4 equal balls. Roll out 2 balls to cover the bottom of 2 cookie sheets. (Note: Cookie sheets should be well-greased.) Mix the filling ingredients together and divide in ½, putting ½ on each cookie sheet. Roll out the other 2 balls of dough and put 1 on each cookie sheet. Mix the remaining milk and sugar together and use to glaze the top layer of dough. Bake at 350° for 30 minutes. For Glaze: Additional ½ c. milk, 2 T. sugar.

APPLESAUCE BROWNIES

1½ C. sugar

½ C. Crisco or margarine

2 eggs

½ tsp. cinnamon

2 T. cocoa

1½ tsp. soda

½ tsp. salt

2 C. flour

1 pt. applesauce

SECOND LAYER:

2 T. sugar

1 C. nuts

1 (12-oz.) pkg. chocolate chips

Cream sugar and margarine. Beat in eggs. Sift dry ingredients and mix alternately with applesauce. Spread mixture in 17x11-inch greased and floured cookie sheet. Mix ingredients for 2nd layer and spread over first. Bake 25-30 minutes at 350°.

PEANUT BUTTER BROWNIES

½ C. butter or margarine (melted)	1 C. flour
1½ C. sugar	½ tsp. salt
½ C. peanut butter	½ tsp. baking powder
1 tsp. vanilla	1 C. nutmeats (optional)
3 eggs	1 C. chocolate baking chips

Mix butter, sugar, peanut butter, vanilla and eggs. Blend in flour, salt and baking powder. Add nutmeats and chocolate chips. Bake in greased 9x13-inch pan at 350° for 30-35 minutes.

QUICK CHERRY BARS

1 C. margarine	3 C. flour
1¾ C. sugar	1½ tsp. baking powder
1 tsp. vanilla	½ tsp. salt
4 eggs	1 can cherry pie filling

Cream margarine and sugar and add vanilla. Add eggs 1 at a time. Add flour, baking powder and salt and mix. Spread all but 1½ C. batter on cookie sheet. Spread pie filling over batter. Then dot remaining batter. Bake at 350°.

164

PUMPKIN BARS

4 eggs
1 C. salad oil
2 C. sugar
1 (15½-oz.) can pumpkin
2 C. flour
2 tsp. baking powder

1 tsp. soda
½ tsp. salt
2 tsp. cinnamon
½ tsp. each of ginger,
cloves and nutmeg

Mix all of the above ingredients and bake at 350° for 25-30 minutes.

FRUIT COCKTAIL BARS

1½ C. sugar
2¼ C. flour
1 can (17-oz.) fruit cocktail and juice

2 eggs
1½ tsp. soda
½ tsp. salt

Put in a bowl and beat. Spread in a jelly roll pan. Bake 30 minutes at 350°. When baked sprinkle on 1½ C. coconut and ½ C. nuts.

FROSTING:
½ C. butter
1 tsp. vanilla

¾ C. sugar
¼ C. evaporated milk

Boil 2 minutes and drizzle over bars.

MARBLED FUDGE BARS

1 C. butter or margarine	1 tsp. vanilla
3 T. cocoa	1 (8-oz.) pkg. cream cheese
2 C. sugar	(softened)
3 eggs	½ C. sugar
½ tsp. salt	1 egg
1 C. flour	1 tsp. vanilla

Melt butter and cocoa. Beat in sugar and eggs until well blended. Stir in flour, salt, vanilla and nuts if desired. Pour into a 9x13-inch pan. Mix the cream cheese, sugar, egg, and vanilla with mixer at low speed until blended, then at medium speed for 2 minutes. With large spoon drop cream cheese in dollops on top of batter. Using tip of knife, lightly score top surface in crisscross pattern. Bake 40-45 minutes at 350°. Cool, cut into bars. Refrigerate.

SPICY RAISIN BARS

1 c. seedless raisins	1 tsp. soda
1 C. water	½ tsp. salt
1 C. sugar	1 tsp. cinnamon
½ C. cooking oil	½ tsp. cloves
1 egg	½ tsp. allspice
1 ¾ C. flour	½ tsp. nutmeg

Combine raisins and water, bring to a boil. Let simmer 5 minutes. Set aside to cool. Mix sugar, oil, and egg. Mix together rest of ingredients. Mix all together with raisins and the water in which they were cooked. Bake in 9x13-inch greased pan in 350° oven. Cool, cut and dust with powdered sugar.

CASHEW COOKIES

1 ½ C. margarine
2 C. browns ugar
1 C. white sugar
3 eggs
1 ½ tsp. vanilla
6 C. flour
2 ¼ tsp. baking powder

2 ½ tsp. baking soda
¾ tsp. salt
1 ½ tsp. cinnamon
¾ tsp. nutmeg
½ pt. sour cream
1 ½ C. cashews (in large chunks)

FROSTING:
1 cube butter
1 ¼ pkgs. powdered sugar

2 tsp. vanilla
Milk

For Cookies: Mix in order given and drop a rounded tablespoon for each cookie as these are large cookies. Bake at 375°-400° for 15-20 minutes. Frost while still warm.

For Frosting: Brown butter, beat in powdered sugar and vanilla and enough milk to make the right consistency for frosting cookies.

DATE COOKIES

1 C. white sugar
1 C. brown sugar
4 C. flour
3 eggs

1 C. butter
1 tsp. soda
1 tsp. vanilla
¼ tsp. salt

DATE FILLING:
1 lb. dates
½ C. flour
½ C. sugar

1 C. hot water
1 C. nuts

Cream sugar into shortening. Add eggs and sifted dry ingredients and vanilla. Roll dough and spread with date filling. For the filling stir all ingredients together. Makes 2 or 3 rolls. Put in refrigerator. Slice and bake as needed.

SUGARLESS BARS

1 C. water
1 C. raisins
2 apples (peeled and cored and cut up into fine pieces)
2 T. liquid sweetener
¼ C. margarine
1 tsp. cinnamon

¼ tsp. nutmeg
1 egg (beaten)
1 C. flour
1 tsp. vanilla
1 tsp. baking soda
½ tsp. walnut flavoring
Pinch of salt

Boil the water, raisins, apples, liquid sweetener, margarine, cinnamon and nutmeg together for 3 minutes and cool. Then add the rest of the ingredients and mix well. Bake in 350° oven for 30 minutes.

DELIGHT COOKIES

1 C. shortening or margarine
1 C. white sugar
1 C. brown sugar
2 eggs
1 tsp. vanilla
2½ C. flour

1 tsp. baking powder
1 tsp. soda
½ tsp. salt
2½ C. oatmeal
2 C. coconut

Cream shortening and sugars. Blend in eggs and vanilla. Sift together flour, baking powder, soda and salt. Add with remaining ingredients. Mix well. Drop by tablespoon onto ungreased cookie sheet. Bake 350°.

GINGERSNAPS

⅔ C. oil
1 C. sugar
1 beaten egg
4 T. light molasses
2 tsp. soda

½ tsp. salt
2½ C. flour
1½ tsp. cinnamon
½ tsp. ginger

Mix oil and sugar. Add beaten eggs. Beat all together well. Stir in molasses, add dry ingredients and mix. Make into small balls, roll in sugar. Bake on ungreased sheet 10 minutes at 350°. They flatten as they bake. Yield depends on size of balls, but usually around 5 doz.

OLD-FASHIONED GINGERSNAP COOKIES

1½ C. sugar
¾ C. shortening
¾ C. molasses or honey
2 eggs
4 tsp. soda

4 C. flour
1 tsp. cinnamon
1 T. ginger
½ tsp. salt

Cream sugar, shortening, molasses or honey and eggs. Add dry ingredients and mix well. Roll into walnut size balls and coat with sugar. Place on greased cookie sheet and bake at 350° for 10 minutes.

BUTTERSCOTCH OATMEAL COOKIES

1½ C. flour
1 tsp. soda
1 C. shortening
¾ C. brown sugar
¾ C. white sugar
2 eggs

1 T. hot water
Walnut meats
6-oz. butterscotch chips
2 C. quick oats
1 tsp. vanilla

Cream shortening and sugars. Add beaten eggs and hot water. Add flour mixed with soda. Add nuts, oatmeal, vanilla and butterscotch chips. Drop by teaspoonful on cookie sheet. Bake 375° for 10-12 minutes.

OATMEAL PLUS COOKIES

1 C. shortening
2 large or 3 small eggs
½ tsp. salt
1 tsp. baking soda
1 C. brown sugar
1 C. white sugar
1 tsp. baking powder
1 tsp. vanilla

1 tsp. maple flavoring
2 C. oatmeal
2 C. flour
2 C. corn flakes (crushed)
1 C. coconut
2 T. milk
Optional: nuts, chocolate chips
        dates or raisins as desired

Mix together all ingredients thoroughly. Drop onto greased cookie sheet. Bake at 350° 12-15 minutes or until lightly browned.

TOFFEE COOKIES

Graham crackers
3 sticks butter (not margarine)
⅔ C. dark brown sugar

1 (12-oz.) pkg. Bits of Brickle
1 (12-oz.) pkg. chocolate chips
Nuts

Line jelly roll pan (10x15) with whole graham crackers. Boil the butter with the dark brown sugar for 3 minutes. Pour over crackers and bake 10 minutes at 350°. Remove from oven and sprinkle with the brickle bits and chocolate chips. Spread and sprinkle with nuts. Cut while warm and remove from pan before completely cool.

SUGAR COOKIES

2 C. margarine
2 C. sugar
2 eggs
4½ C. flour

1 tsp. soda
½ tsp. salt
Vanilla

Mix and chill. Roll into small balls; dip in sugar, flatten with a fork. Bake 350° for 12-15 minutes.

SUGAR COOKIES

4 ½ C. flour	1 C. oil
1 C. granulated sugar	2 eggs
1 C. powdered sugar	1 tsp. baking soda
1 tsp. salt	1 tsp. cream of tartar
1 C. butter or margarine	1 tsp. vanilla

Cream butter, salad oil, powdered sugar, granulated sugar until light and fluffy; add eggs and vanilla and continue beating, scraping sides of bowl. Gradually add dry ingredients and continue mixing until well mixed. Cover with wax paper and refrigerate for 2 hours or overnight. Grease cookie sheet; roll dough into balls and after putting on cookie sheet, press each with a fork. Makes about 12 doz. cookies. Bake at 350° for about 8-10 minutes or until light brown. To make filled cookies, put any kind of jam in the center of one cookie then put another cookie on top and press the edges together with a fork.

REFRIGERATOR DATE COOKIES

1 C. Crisco	1 C. dates
2 C. brown sugar	1 tsp. salt
2 eggs	1 tsp. soda
1 C. nuts	3 ½ C. cake flour

Cream Crisco and sifted brown sugar. Add eggs 1 at a time and beat well after each. Add nuts and dates. Sift dry ingredients and add to creamed mixture. Shape into rolls, wrap in waxed paper and store in refrigerator until firm. Slice and bake 8 minutes at 400°.

ALMOND-SPICE OATMEAL COOKIES

1 C. brown sugar
1 C. margarine (softened)
1 egg
1½ C. quick-cooking oats
1½ C. flour

½ tsp. baking soda
½ tsp. salt
½ tsp. cinnamon
¼ tsp. cloves
¼ tsp. allspice

Mix brown sugar, margarine and egg thoroughly. Stir in rest of ingredients. Shape dough by tablespoonful in 1½-inch balls. Place 1-inch apart on ungreased cookie sheet. Press down with a fork. Bake at 375° oven 8-10 minutes or until no indentation remains when touched. Cool slightly and remove from sheet. Spread with glaze: 1 C. powdered sugar, 2 tsp. margarine, softened; ¼ tsp. almond flavoring. Mix until smooth. Makes 2½ doz.

PECAN TASSIES

FILLING:
2 eggs (beaten)
1½ C. brown sugar
2 T. soft margarine

2 tsp. vanilla
1 C. chopped pecans
Salt

CRUST:
3-oz. cream cheese
½ C. butter

1 C. flour

Soften cream cheese and butter; blend in flour. Chill 1 hour; roll 1/8-inch thick and cut with 3-inch cutter. Place in ungreased small muffin pan. Blend filling ingredients. Put 1 teaspoonful in each cup. Bake at 325° for 20-25 minutes.

FRENCH COOKIES

1 lb. butter	6 C. flour
3 C. sugar	6 eggs
½ tsp. cinnamon	

Cream butter and sugar thoroughly; add egg yolks (beaten light and fluffy). Add sifted flour and cinnamon; then add stiffly beaten egg whites and mix thoroughly. Batter will be thick. Drop by teaspoonful onto a hot waffle iron and bake 1½-2 minutes. Cookies will be hard but will soften on being left in cookie jar. Can be baked a couple of weeks ahead of time of use.

PEANUT BUTTER COOKIES

½ C. shortening	½ C. peanut butter
½ C. white sugar	1¼ C. flour
½ C. brown sugar	½ tsp. soda
1 egg	¼ tsp. salt
2 T. hot water	

Mix all ingredients together. Shape into balls and press fork on top to make design. Bake 10-12 minutes in a 350° oven.

COCONUT BON BONS

1 stick margarine (melted)
1 can Eagle Brand milk
2 lb. powdered sugar
½ cake paraffin

1 C. nutmeats
1 T. vanilla
1 (14-oz.) pkg. coconut
12-oz. pkg. chocolate chips

Combine ingredients; mix well. Shape into small balls. Put on cookie sheet and chill. Melt ½ cake paraffin and 12-oz. pkg. chocolate chips in double boiler; insert toothpicks in bon bons and dip in chocolate. Put on waxed paper to cool and harden.

CHOCOLATE DROP COOKIES

1 C. margarine or butter
2 C. sugar
2 eggs
1½ C. buttermilk or sour milk
2 tsp. vanilla

3½ C. sifted flour
1 tsp. soda
1 tsp. salt
1 C. cocoa
Nuts

FROSTING:
2 T. butter
2 (2-oz.) sq. chocolate

3 T. warm water
2 C. powdered sugar

Mix thoroughly butter, sugar, and eggs. Stir in buttermilk and vanilla. Sift together and stir in flour, soda, salt, cocoa, and nuts. Chill and drop by teaspoonful about 2-inches apart on lightly greased sheet. Bake 350° for 8-10 minutes. Melt butter, chocolate, and blend in water and powdered sugar. Frost.

BUTTER PECAN COOKIES

1 C. butter
½ C. brown sugar
1 egg yolk

2 C. (or more) flour
¼ tsp. salt

TOPPING:
½ egg
2 T. milk

60 pecans

Cream butter until light and fluffy. Add to sugar gradually and cream well. Add unbeaten egg yolk and blend thoroughly. Add flour and salt. Fold into mixture. If sticky, add more flour. Roll in ball size of marble and put on greased cookie sheet. Press down with fork dipped in egg-milk mixture. Place pecan on each. Bake at 350° for 12-15 minutes. Yields: 60 cookies.

PEANUT BUTTER BARS

½ C. margarine
½ C. granulated sugar
½ C. brown sugar
1 egg
⅓ C. peanut butter

½ tsp. soda
¼ tsp. salt
½ tsp. vanilla
1 C. flour
1 C. rolled oats

Cream margarine and sugars. Blend in egg, peanut butter, soda, salt, and vanilla. Stir in flour and rolled oats. Spread in greased 9x13-inch pan. Bake at 350° for 20-25 minutes. Sprinkle with 1 C. (6-oz.) chocolate chips; let stand 5 minutes and spread over cookies. Combine ½ C. sifted powdered sugar, ¼ C. peanut butter and 2-4 T. milk. Spread over top of chocolate chips or drizzle on. Cool and cut into bars.

RHUBARB BARS

3 C. rhubarb
1½ C. sugar
2 tsp. cornstarch
¼ C. water
1 tsp. vanilla
1½ C. oatmeal

1½ C. flour
1 C. shortening (part butter)
1 C. brown sugar
½ tsp. soda
½ C. nuts (chopped)

Dissolve cornstarch in water. Mix rhubarb, sugar, cornstarch dissolved in water and vanilla and cook until thickened. Mix oatmeal, flour, shortening, brown sugar, soda and nuts together until crumbly. Pat ¾ of mixture in 9x13-inch pan. Pour in the rhubarb mixture and sprinkle remaining crumb mixture on top. Bake at 375° for 30-35 minutes.

BUTTERSCOTCH COOKIES

CREAM:
1 C. brown sugar
1 C. white sugar
1½ C. shortening
ADD:
2 beaten eggs
2 tsp. soda dissolved in
2 T. vinegar

SIFT:
2 tsp. baking powder
4 C. flour
¼ tsp. salt
ADD:
1 tsp. vanilla
1 tsp. almond extract

Roll in balls and press with fork. Bake 350° until light brown. Makes about 7 doz. small cookies. May be stored in refrigerator in tight container.

BAVARIAN MINT CHIPPERS

1 C. soft margarine	½-¾ tsp. mint extract
¾ C. sugar	2½ C. flour
¾ C. brown sugar	1 tsp. soda
2 eggs	1 tsp. salt
2 tsp. instant coffee	2 C. chocolate chips
dissolved in 1 T. hot water	1 C. chopped nuts

Cream margarine and sugars. Add 2 eggs and mix well. Add dissolved coffee. Add dry ingredients and mix well. Add chips and nuts and mix well. Bake as usual.

YUM YUM BARS

1 pkg. (14-oz.) caramels	1 stick margarine (melted)
⅔ C. evaporated milk	½ C. walnuts (chopped)
1 German chocolate cake mix	1 pkg. (6-oz.) chocolate chips

Melt caramels and ⅓ C. evaporated milk in double boiler. Mix dry cake mix, ⅓ C. evaporated milk, margarine and nuts. Press ½ in 9x13-inch pan and bake 6 minutes at 350°. Remove from oven and sprinkle on chocolate chips and drizzle on melted caramels. Dot with remaining cake mixture. Bake another 15-18 minutes. Cool. Cut in small squares.

BROWNIES

14-oz. pkg. caramels
⅔ C. evaporated milk
1 pkg. German chocolate cake mix

¾ C. margarine (melted)
1 C. nutmeats (chopped)
1 C. chocolate chips

Heat caramels with ⅓ C. milk to melt; set aside. Combine cake mix, margarine and remaining ⅓ C. milk; mix well and add nutmeats. Press ½ the dough into greased 9x13-inch pan. Bake 5-10 minutes at 350°. Remove from oven and sprinkle with chocolate chips. Pour melted caramel mixture over chips. Spoon on remaining dough. Bake 20 minutes at 350°.

LEMON COCONUT SQUARES

CRUST:
1 ½ C. flour
½ C. brown sugar

½ C. butter or margarine

FILLING:
2 beaten eggs
1 C. brown sugar (packed)
1 ½ C. coconut
1 C. chopped nuts

2 T. flour
½ tsp. baking powder
¼ tsp. salt
½ tsp. vanilla

ICING:
1 C. powdered sugar
1 T. melted butter

Juice of 1 lemon

Mix flour, brown sugar, sugar and margarine together and pat down into a buttered 9x13-inch pan. Bake slowly in a 275° oven. Combine filling ingredients together and spread on top of baked mixture. Bake 20 minutes in a 350° oven. While warm spread icing over top.

FUDGEY BROWNIE (MIXES IN 5 MINUTES)

¾ C. cocoa
½ tsp. soda
⅔ C. vegetable oil
½ C. boiling water
  (measure accurately)

2 C. sugar
2 eggs
1⅓ C. unsifted flour
1 tsp. vanilla
¼ tsp. salt

Stir cocoa and soda in mixing bowl. Blend in ⅓ C. oil. Add boiling water; stir until mix thickens. Stir in sugar, eggs and remaining ⅓ C. oil; stir until smooth. Add flour, vanilla, salt, blend completely. Pour into lightly greased 9x13-inch pan or two 8x8-inch square pans. Bake at 350° for 35-40 minutes for 9x13-inch pan or 30-32 minutes for 8x8-inch pans. Cool and frost if desired.

APPLE BARS

2 C. white sugar
1½ C. oil
2 eggs
3 C. diced apples
2 tsp. vanilla

3 C. flour
1 tsp. soda
1 tsp. salt
1 tsp. cinnamon

Mix all ingredients together and pour into jelly roll pan, sprinkle top with ½ C. brown sugar. Bake at 350° for 30-35 minutes.

CANDY

BROWN SUGAR NUT ROLL

2 C. granulated sugar
1 C. brown sugar
1 C. evaporated milk

¼ C. corn syrup
Dash salt
1 C. chopped pecans

Butter sides of heavy 2-qt. saucepan. In it combine sugars, milk, corn syrup and salt. Stir over medium heat until sugars dissolve. Cook to soft ball stage (236°). Stir often. Immediately remove from heat. Cool to lukewarm (110°). Do not stir. Beat until fudge begins to hold its shape. Turn out on buttered surface. Knead fudge until it can be shaped, keeping hands well buttered. Shape in two 7-inch rolls and roll immediately in chopped nuts. Wrap in foil or waxed paper. Chill until ready to slice. Cut in ½-inch slices. Makes about 28 pieces of candy. (NOTE: Mixture will curdle while cooking but becomes smooth when you beat it.)

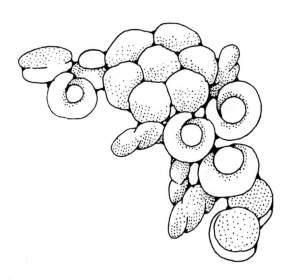

APRICOT COCONUT BALLS

1½ C. (6-oz.) dried apricots (ground)
2 C. moist shredded coconut
Confectioner's sugar (if desired)

⅔ C. (½ can or 7½-oz.) Eagle
Brand sweetened condensed
milk

In large sized mixing bowl blend together apricots and coconut. Stir in Eagle Brand sweetened condensed milk. Shape into small balls and roll in sugar. Let stand in air until firm. Makes about 1½ doz. 1¼-inch diameter candies.

DATE CANDY

1½ C. chopped dates
3 C. sugar
3 T. white syrup

1-2 C. chopped nuts
1 C. evaporated milk
¼ C. margarine

Cook dates, sugar, syrup, milk, and margarine to a soft ball stage, stirring constantly. Remove from heat and cool. Add nuts and beat as long as you can. Put on a cutting board covered with powdered sugar. Roll and shape into a roll about the size of Pella Bologna and slice into ¼-inch pieces.

CRISPIX CHOCOLATE DROPS

1 pkg. (12-oz., 2 C.) butterscotch
   morsels
1 pkg. (6-oz., 1 C.) semi-sweet
   chocolate morsels

1½ C. salted peanuts
4 C. Crispix cereal

Combine butterscotch morsels and semi-sweet chocolate morsels in large saucepan. Stir constantly over very low heat until smooth. Remove from heat. Add peanuts and Crispix. Stir gently until well coated. Drop by teaspoonful onto waxed paper. Chill until firm. Yield 8 doz.

NO-BAKE PEANUT CLUSTERS

Mix in saucepan:

½ C. chocolate bits   ½ C. flour
¼ C. milk   ½ stick margarine
¾ C. sugar

Place over medium heat and cook for 2 minutes after bubbles appear, stirring constantly. Remove from heat and stir in: ⅓ C. quick cooking oatmeal, ¼ C. peanut
butter, ½ tsp.. vanilla, 1 C. dry roasted peanuts. Drop by rounded teaspoons onto
waxed paper for cookie size. Yield 2 doz. Will make about 40 candy size pieces.

PEANUT BUTTER CARAMEL CORN

12 C. popped corn   ½ C. honey
    (without oil)   ½ C. white syrup
Salted peanuts   1 C. peanut butter
1 C. sugar   1 tsp. vanilla

Boil sugar, syrup, and honey 3 minutes, ONLY; NO LONGER, only if a crisper caramel
is desired. Blend the peanut butter and vanilla into hot syrup and pour this over
the popped corn and nuts and stir until well coated. Captain Crunch cereal (1½
boxes) is very good as a substitute for corn.

ENGLISH TOFFEE

½ lb. butter
1 C. sugar
3 T. cold water

1 tsp. vanilla
8 small Hershey bars (cut up)

Cook butter, sugar and cold water until mixture is the color of coffee with cream. Use a heavy pan and stir constantly. Add vanilla and stir. Pour on a buttered cookie sheet. Spread out over all the pan. Place the cut up Hershey bars on the hot toffee. Let them melt and spread with a knife. Chill. Break into pieces. Do not put in a plastic container, as it will soften.

ROCK CANDY

2 C. sugar
½ C. light syrup
½ C. water
Pinch of salt

Food coloring (opt.)
4-6 drops flavoring (anise,
    wintergreen or peppermint)

Combine sugar, syrup, water, salt; bring to a boil. Cook to hard crack stage; add color and flavoring. Pour into buttered pan and let set until firm.

POPCORN BALLS

1 C. sugar   ½ tsp. salt
⅓ C. white corn syrup   ¾ tsp. vanilla
⅓ C. water   4-5 qts. popped corn
4 T. butter

Cook sugar, water, syrup, salt and butter until syrup forms a brittle ball in cold water. Pour over popped corn and stir well. Let stand a few minutes. Butter hands and make into balls.

PEANUT BUTTER FUDGE

¾ lb. butter or margarine   6 T. cocoa
¾ C. chunky peanut butter   1¼ boxes powdered sugar
1½ T. vanilla

In microwave oven or stove top, melt margarine and peanut butter. Remove from heat, add cocoa, and vanilla and mix well. Add powdered sugar. Have a buttered 9x13-inch pan ready as fudge sets up very quickly. Cut into squares when cool.

FIDDLE FADDLE CORN

1 ½ C. white sugar
1 ½ C. brown sugar
½ C. Carnation milk

½ C. milk
½ C. butter
2 tsp. vanilla

Boil ingredients to 248° (soft ball stage). Pour over 5-6-qts. popped corn and stir thoroughly.

DIVINITY

3 C. sugar
½ C. syrup
½ C. water

2 egg whites
1 tsp. vanilla
Nuts (opt.)

Combine sugar, syrup and water in saucepan and bring to soft ball stage. Add slowly ½ to stiffly beaten egg whites while beating constantly. Stop beating and bring last ½ of syrup to hard ball stage. Add slowly to egg white mix while beating constantly. Continue beating until it starts to lose its gloss. Add vanilla and nuts. Dip by teaspoonful onto waxed paper. About 30 minutes total preparation. Makes 36 pieces.

For Cocoa Divinity: Melt ⅔ C. shortening, stir in ½ C. cocoa. Keep warm over warm water until candy is ready to dip, then quickly stir in chocolate mix. May add ½ tsp. almond flavor if desired.

HELPFUL HINTS

HELPFUL HINTS

Hair spray (the inexpensive kinds) is good for removing ball point pen ink from clothes. Spray well immediately before washing as usual.

Rags soaked well in strong solution of cayenne pepper is a good thing to put in mice and rat holes.

Lighter fluid is good for removing cosmetic stains in clothing. Just spot spray before washing as usual. Also use to remove gum from clothes and hair.

Sprinkle cayenne in ant and roach runs.

If you have a bothersome tickling cough, try chewing slightly on a whole clove. It also helps sweeten the breath.

When several vehicles are stopped at sign or signal, allow enough distance so that you see the rear tires of the vehicle ahead of you, to avoid you being pushed into vehicle ahead of you should you be hit in the rear.

When bread is baking, a small dish of water in oven will help keep crust from getting hard.

For flakier pastry, add 1 teaspoon vinegar to cold water when preparing.

Three pounds dry navy beans equals 1 gallon baked beans.

Club soda substituted for liquid in a pancake recipe encourages a light texture.

Add a teaspoon of vinegar to cooked icing. This will keep it from cracking when it is cut.

When creaming butter and sugar for a cake, add a little hot water to milk, makes a finer textured cake and easier creaming.

Brush the inside of your bottom crust with egg white when making fruit pies. This prevents juice from soaking through.

To cut fresh cake, use a thin, sharp knife, dipped in water.

Roll biscuit dough thin, then fold it before cutting. Makes them flaky in center and split open easily for buttering.

Add a pinch of salt to Jell-o, improves the flavor.

Brush cream, then sprinkle sugar on top of two crust pie. . . browns beautifully.

Keep a toothbrush around the kitchen sink. . .you will find it useful in cleaning rotary beaters, graters and choppers.

When your hands are badly stained from gardening add a teaspoon of sugar to the soapy lather you wash them in.

Before emptying the bag of your vacuum cleaner, sprinkle water on the newspaper into which it is emptied and there will be no scattering of dust.

Plant a few sprigs of dill near your tomato plants to prevent tomato worms on your plants.

Marigolds will prevent rodents.

Spray garbage sacks with ammonia to prevent dogs from tearing the bags before picked up.

You can clean darkened aluminum pans easily by boiling in them two teaspoons of cream of tartar mixed in a quart of water.

Try waxing your ashtrays. Ashes won't cling. . .odors won't linger and they can be wiped clean with a paper towel or disposable tissue.

Fresh lemon juice will take away onion scent from hands.

Wash old powder puffs in soapy water, rinse well and dry thoroughly. Then use them for polishing silverware, copper and brass.

Never beat egg whites in an aluminum pan, it is sure to darken them.

Add one teaspoon of soda to cranberries while cooking them and they will not require as much sugar.

To whiten piano keys, wash them with alcohol.

Do not put oils on vinyl furniture. It will cause it to harden. To clean, wash with mild detergent and wipe dry.

To avoid steaming up the entire bathroom run cool water in tub first, then add the hot.

If paste isn't available, the white of an egg will do.

To cut a pie into five equal pieces, slice a Y in the pie and then slice the two larger pieces in half.

Don't dispose of circular cardboard backs from frozen pizzas. Cover with foil and use as plates when taking round cakes away from home.

When shoestrings lose their plastic tips, dip the ends in clear fingernail polish.

When tying up a package for mailing, wet the cords, they tighten as they dry, holding the package more securely.

You'll have delicious golden fried potatoes if you sprinkle them lightly with flour before frying.

Rub chigger bites with an aspirin tablet, slightly dampened.

To cut fresh bread easily, cut with a hot knife.

Put a layer of marshmallows in the bottom of a pumpkin pie, then add the filling. You will have a nice topping as the marshmallows will come to the top.

Place your new nylons in a baggie and put in the freezer. They will last much longer.

Meatloaf will not stick to the pan if you place a strip or two of bacon at the bottom of the pan before packing the meat in.

Instead of using expensive household window cleaner, buy car windshield solvent and use in a spray bottle.

Chilled cheese grates more easily.

Experienced cooks do a roast with the fat side up. . .that way the juice soaks down into the meat and keeps it moist.

To clean hair brushes, rinse them thoroughly in cold water to which a generous amount of ammonia has been added; then shake and place in the open air to dry. The ammonia removes the dirt like magic.

HANDY CHART OF KITCHEN MATH
(Size of Pans and Baking Dishes)

Cooking need never become a crisis, when you use our handy charts. Need a 4 or 6-cup baking dish? Will your fancy mold be the right size for the recipe? See below for the answers.

COMMON KITCHEN PANS TO USE AS CASSEROLES

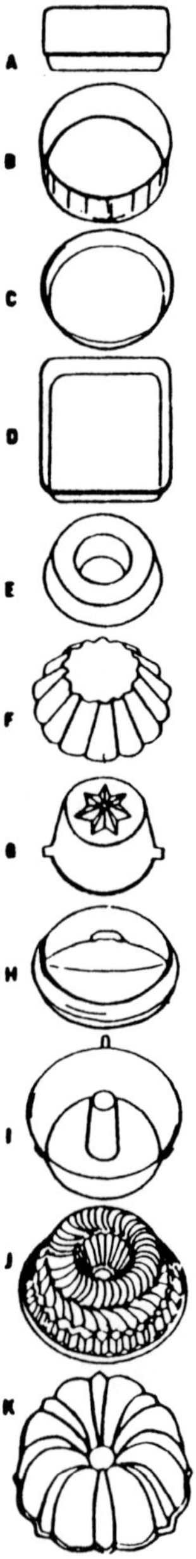

WHEN THE RECIPES CALLS FOR:

4-Cup Baking Dish:
9-inch pie plate
8 x 1¼-inch layer-cake pan - **C**
7 3/8 x 3 5/8 x 2¼-inch loaf pan - **A**

6-Cup Baking Dish:
8 or 9 x 11½-inch layer-cake pan - **C**
10-inch pie plate
8½ x 3 5/8 x 2 5/8-inch loaf pan - **A**

8-Cup Baking Dish:
8 x 8 x 2-inch square pan - **D**
11 x 7 x 1½-inch baking pan
9 x 5 x 3-inch loaf pan - **A**

10-Cup Baking Dish:
9 x 9 x 2-inch square pan
11¾ x 7½ x 1¾-inch baking pan - **D**
15 x 10 x 1-inch jelly-roll pan

12-Cup Baking Dish Or Over:

13½ x 8½ x 2-inch glass baking pan	12 cups
13 x 9 x 2-inch metal baking pan	15 cups
14 x 10½ x 2½-inch roasting pan	19 cups

TOTAL VOLUME OF VARIOUS SPECIAL BAKING PANS

Tube Pans:

7½ x 3-inch "Bundt" tube - **K**	6 cups
9 x 3½-inch fancy tube or "Bundt" pan - **J OR K**	9 cups
9 x 3½-inch angel cake pan - **I**	12 cups
10 X 3¾-inch "Bundt" or "Crownburst" pan - **K**	12 cups
9 x 3½-inch fancy tube - **J**	12 cups
10 x 4-inch fancy tube mold (kugelhupf) - **J**	16 cups
10 x 4-inch angel food pan - **I**	18 cups

Melon Mold:

7 x 5½ x 4-inch mold - **H**	6 cups

Spring-Form Pans:

8 x 3-inch pan - **B**	12 cups
9 x 3-inch pan - **B**	16 cups

Ring Molds:

8½ x 2¼-inch mold - **E**	4½ cups
9¼ x 2¾-inch mold - **E**	8 cups

Charlotte Mold:

6 x 4¼-inch mold - **G**	7½ cups

Brioche Pan:

9½ x 3¼-inch pan - **F**	8 cups

194

BAKING TEMPERATURES AND TIMES

Breads

Baking Powder Biscuits	450°F. 12-15 min.
Muffins	400°-425°F. 20-25 min.
Quick Breads	350°F. 40-60 min.
Yeast Bread	375°-400°F. 45-60 min.
Yeast Rolls	400°F. 15-20 min.

Cakes

Butter Loaf Cakes	350°F. 45-60 min.
Butter Layer Cakes	350°-375°F. 25-35 min.
Cupcakes	375°F. 20-25 min.
Chiffon Cakes	325°F. 60 min.
Sponge Cakes	325°F. 60 min.
Angel Food Cakes	325°F. 60 min.

Cookies

Bar Cookies	350°F. 25-30 min.
Drop Cookies	350°-375°F. 8-12 min.
Rolled and Ref. Cookies	350°-400°F. 8-12 min.

Pastry

Meringues	350°F. 12-20 min.
Pie Shells	450°F. 12-15 min.
Filled Pies	450°F. 10 min. lower to 350°F. 40 min.

Roasts

Beef Roast	325°F. Rare 18-20 min. per lb.
	Medium 22-25 min. per lb.
	Well done -30 min. per lb.
Chicken	325°F-350°F. 30 min. per lb.
Duck	325°F-350°F. 25 min. per lb.
Fish Fillets	500°F. 15-20 min.
Goose	325°F-350°F. 30 min. per lb.
Ham	350°F. 20-30 min. per lb.
Lamb	300°F-350°F. 35 min. per lb.
Meat loaf	375°F. 60 min. for 2 lb. loaf
Pork Roast	350°F. 30 min. per lb.
Turkey	250°F-325°F. 15-25 min. per lb.
Veal Roast	300°F. 30 min. per lb.
Venison	350°F. 20-25 min. per lb.

TEMPERATURE TESTS FOR CANDY MAKING

There are two different methods of determining when candy has been cooked to the proper consistency. One is by using a candy thermometer in order to record degrees, the other is by using the cold water test. The chart below will prove useful in helping to follow candy recipes:

TYPE OF CANDY	DEGREES	COLD WATER
Fondant, Fudge	234-238°	Soft Ball
Divinity	245-248°	Firm Ball
Taffy	265-270°	Hard Ball
Butterscotch	275-280°	Light Crack
Peanut Brittle	285-290°	Hard Crack
Caramelized Sugar	310-321°	Caramelized

In using the cold water test, use a fresh cupful of cold water for each test. When testing, remove the candy from the fire and pour aobut ½ teaspoon of candy into the cold water. Pick the candy up in the fingers and roll into a ball if possible.

In the SOFT BALL TEST the candy will roll into a soft ball which quickly loses its shape when removed from the water.

In the FIRM BALL TEST the candy will roll into a firm ball but not hard ball. It will flatten out a few minutes after being removed from water.

In the HARD BALL TEST the candy will roll into a hard ball which has lost almost all plasticity and will roll around on a plate on removal from the water.

In the LIGHT CRACK TEST the candy will form brittle threads which will soften on removal from the water.

In the HARD CRACK TEST the candy will form brittle threads in the water which will remain brittle after being removed from the water.

In CARAMELIZING, the sugar first melts then becomes a golden brown. It will form a hard brittle ball in cold water.

QUANTITIES OF FOODS CHARTS

Food	Amount Before Preparation	Amount After Preparation
CEREALS:		
Macaroni	1 C. (3½ oz.)	2½ C. cooked
Noodles, medium	3 C. (4 oz.)	3 C. cooked
Spaghetti	8 oz.	4 C. cooked
Long grain rice	1 C. (7 oz.)	3 C. cooked
Quick-cooking rice	1 C. (3 oz.)	2 C. cooked
Popcorn	¼ C.	5 C. popped
CRUMBS:		
Bread	1 slice	¾ C. soft or ¼ C. fine dry crumbs
Saltine crackers	28 crackers	1 C. finely crushed
Rich ground crackers	24 crackers	1 C. finely crushed
Graham crackers	14 squares	1 C. finely crushed
Gingersnaps	15 cookies	1 C. finely crushed
Vanilla wafers	22 cookies	1 C. finely crushed
FRUITS:		
Apples	1 medium	1 C. sliced
Bananas	1 medium	⅓ C. mashed
Cherries, dark sweet	1 lb.	2 C. pitted
Cranberries	1 lb. (4 C.)	3 C. sauce
Lemons	1 medium	3 T. juice; 2 tsp. shredded peel
Limes	1 medium	2 T. juice; 1½ tsp. shredded peel
Oranges	1 medium	¼-⅓ C. juice; 4 tsp. shredded peel
Peaches, pears	1 medium	½ C. sliced
Strawberries	4 C. whole	3½ C. sliced
VEGETABLES:		
Beans, dry	1 lb. (2½ C.)	6 C. cooked
Cabbage	1 lb. (1 small)	5 C. shredded
Carrots, without tops	1 lb. (6-8 medium)	3 C. shredded or 2½ C. chopped
Celery	1 medium bunch	4½ C. chopped
Green beans, cut up	1 lb. (3 C.)	2½ C. cooked
Green peppers	1 large	1 C. chopped
Mushrooms	1 lb. (6 C.)	2 C. sliced and cooked
Onions	1 medium	½ C. chopped
Potatoes	1 medium	⅔ C. cubed or ½ C. mashed
Spinach	1 lb. (12 C.)	1½ C. cooked
Tomatoes	1 medium	½ C. cooked
NUTS:		
Almonds	1 lb. in shell	1¼ C. shelled
Pecans	1 lb. in shell	2 C. shelled
Walnuts	1 lb. in shell	1½ C. shelled
MISCELLANEOUS:		
Eggs	4 whole, 8 yolks, or 8 whites	1 C.
Cheese	4 oz.	1 C. shredded
Whipping Cream	1 C.	2 C. whipped
Boneless raw meat	1 lb.	2 C. cooked and chopped
Cooked meat	1 lb.	3 C. chopped

197

HAM LOAF FOR 100

16 lbs. cured ham (ground)
8 lb. ground beef
20 eggs
2 ¼ qts. tomato juice (or milk)

2 ¼ qts. cracker crumbs
2 T. salt
2 tsp. pepper
2 tsp. dry mustard

Mix all together and bake at 350°.

AMOUNTS TO BUY FOR A CROWD

BEVERAGES	For 50 Servings	Size of ea. serving
Coffee, instant	1 (6 oz.) jar	¾ C.
Coffee, regular	1-1 ¼ lb.	¾ C.
Tea	¼ lb.	¾ C.
Fruit juice, frozen concentrate	9 (6 oz.) cans	½ C.
Fruit or tomato juice (canned)	4 (46 oz.) cans	½ C.
Lemonade concentrate (frozen)	13 (6 oz.) cans	1 C.
Punch	2 gallons	⅔ C.
MEAT, POULTRY, FISH		
Bacon	6 lbs.	2 slices
Beef, rolled	25 lbs.	½ lb.
Beef, standing rib roast	35 lbs.	¾ lbs.
Chicken, to roast	35 to 40 lbs.	¾ lbs.
Chicken, stewing, for cutting up	20 to 25 lbs.	
Ham, canned, boned	1 (14 lb. can)	¼ lb.
Ham, bone in	22 to 25 lbs.	⅓ lb.
Hamburger	12 ½ to 15 lbs.	4 to 5 oz. patty
Meat, ground for meat loaf	12 lbs.	¼ lb. meat
Pork chops	17 lbs.	1 chop ¾'' thick
VEGETABLES		
Canned vegetables	14 No. 303 cans	or 11 No. 2 cans
Frozen vegetables	13-17 oz. pkgs.	½ C.
Potatoes, for creaming	12 ½ to 15 lbs.	½ C.
French fries, frozen	16 (9 oz.) pkgs.	About 3 oz.
Potatoes (mashed)	25 lbs.	½ C.
RELISHES AND SALADS		
Cabbage, for slaw	12 to 15 lbs.	⅓ C.
Lettuce, for lettuce hearts	12 medium heads	1/5 head
Lettuce, leaf for salad	6 heads	2 or 3 leaves
Fruit salad	9 qts.	¾ C.
Tomatoes, for salad	30 med.	3 slices
MISCELLANEOUS		
Bread	5 (1 lb.) loaves	1 ½ slices
Butter or margarine	1 to 1 ¼ lb.	1 pat, ½'' thick
Ice cream	2 to 2 ½ gal.	1 slice or 1 scoop

EMERGENCY SUBSTITUTIONS

Here, then, we offer a guide that we hope will be handy - in a pinch.

For these:	You may use these:
1 tsp. baking powder	1 tsp. cream of tartar plus 1 tsp. baking soda
1 C. butter	1 C. margarine or 1 C. hydrogenated fat or lard plus ½ tsp. salt
1 sq. (1 oz.) chocolate	3 T. cocoa powder plus 1 T. fat
1 T. cornstarch	2 T. flour
1 tsp. flour (for thickening)	½ tsp. cornstarch or 2 tsp. quick-cooking tapioca
1 C. all-purpose flour	1 C. plus 2 T. cake flour
1 C. cake flour	7/8 C. all-purpose flour
1 C. sour milk or buttermilk	1 C. milk plus 1 T. lemon juice or vinegar
1 C. fresh whole milk	½ C. evaporated milk plus ½ C. water
1 C. skim milk	4 T. nonfat dry milk plus 1 C. water
1 C. honey	1¼ C. sugar plus ¼ C. liquid
1½ C. corn syrup	1 C. sugar plus ¼ C. water
¼ C. cinnamon sugar	¼ C. granulated sugar plus 1 tsp. cinnamon
1 cake compressed yeast	1 pkg. or 1 T. (scant) active dry yeast
1 C. tomato juice	½ C. tomato sauce plus ½ C. water
1 C. ketchup or chili sauce	1 C. tomato sauce plus ½ C. sugar plus 2 T. vinegar
15-oz. can tomato sauce	6-oz. can tomato paste plus 1 C. water
16-oz. can tomatoes, cut up	3 fresh medium tomatoes, cut up
15-oz. can spaghetti sauce	2 C. pizza sauce or Italian cooking sauce

1 C. fine dry bread crumbs	1 C. crushed cereal or cracker crumbs
1 T. snipped fresh herbs	1 tsp. dried herbs, crushed
1 medium onion	1 T. minced dried onion
8-oz. carton dairy sour cream	8-oz. carton plain yogurt
1 C. light cream	1 C. undiluted evaporated milk
1 C. whipped cream, whipped	4-oz. container frozen whipped dessert topping, thawed

FOOD EQUIVALENTS

This amount:	Equals this amount:
1 slice soft bread	½ C. soft crumbs
1 slice dry bread crumbs	⅓ C. fine dry bread crumbs
1 lb. butter or margarine	2 C.
1 lb. hydrogenated shortening	2⅓ C.
1 lb. rolled oats	6¼ C.; 8 C. cooked
1 lb. long-grain rice	2½ C.; about 8 C. cooked
½ lb. pre-cooked rice	2 C.
1 lb. cheddar, American, Anerican, Swiss or mozzarella cheese	4 C. grated
1 lb. cottage cheese	2 C.
8 oz. cream cheese	1 C.
3 oz. cream cheese	6 T. (about ⅓ C.)
3 oz. parmesan cheese	1 C. grated or shredded
6 oz. chocolate chips	1 C.
1 oz. unsweetened chocolate	1 square
1 lb. cocoa	4 C. ground
1 lb. coffee	5 C. ground
1 lb. corn meal	3 C.
23 soda crackers, ground	1 C.
15 graham crackers, ground	1 C.
1 egg	4 T. liquid
4-5 whole eggs	1 C.
7-9 egg whites	1 C.
12-14 yolks	1 C.

1 lb. all-purpose flour	4 C.
1 lb. cake flour	4½ C.
1 lb. graham flour	3½ C.
1 medium lemon	2-3 T. juice
1 medium orange	2-3 T. juice
3-4 medium oranges	1 C. juice
1 lb. brown sugar	2½ C.
1 lb. granulated sugar	2½ C.
1 lb. powdered sugar	3½ C.
1 lb. white potatoes	3 medium; 2¼ C. cooked; 1¾ C. mashed
8 oz. macaroni, spaghetti, noodles	4 C. cooked

Sometimes if you're using recipes from older cookbooks, the oven temperatures are given as "moderate", "slow", or "hot". It's a shame not to use these recipes just because you're not sure of the temperature. This guide should give you some direction:

OVEN TEMPERATURE GUIDE

Very slow	250°-275°F.
Slow	300°-325°F.
Moderate	350°-375°F.
Hot	400°-425°F.
Very hot	450°-475°F
Extremely hot	500°-525°F.

WEIGHTS AND MEASURES

Standard Abbreviations

t. — teaspoon
T. — tablespoon
c. — cup
f.g. — few grains
pt. — pint
qt. — quart

d.b. — double boiler
B.P. — baking powder
oz. — ounce
lb. — pound
pk. — peck
bu. — bushel

Guide to Weights and Measures

1 teaspoon - 60 drops
3 teaspoons - 1 tablespoon
2 tablespoons - 1 fluid ounce
4 tablespoons - ¼ cup
5¹/₃ tablespoons - ¹/₃ cup
8 tablespoons - ½ cup
16 tablespoons - 1 cup

1 pound - 16 ounces
1 cup - ½ pint
2 cups - 1 pint
4 cups - 1 quart
4 quarts - 1 gallon
8 quarts - 1 peck
4 pecks - 1 bushel

Substitutions and Equivalents

2 tablespoons of fat - 1 ounce
1 cup of fat - ½ pound
1 pound of butter - 2 cups
1 cup of hydrogenated fat plus ½ t. salt - 1 cup butter
2 cups sugar - 1 pound
2½ cups packed brown sugar - 1 pound
1¹/₃ cups packed brown sugar - 1 cup of granulated sugar
3½ cups of powdered sugar - 1 pound
4 cups sifted all purpose flour - 1 pound
4½ cups sifted cake flour - 1 pound
1 ounce bitter chocolate - 1 square
4 tablespoons cocoa plus 2 teaspoons butter - 1 ounce of bitter chocolate
1 cup egg whites - 8 to 10 whites
1 cup egg yolks - 12 to 14 yolks
16 marshmallows - ¼ pound
1 tablespoon cornstarch - 2 tablespoons flour for thickening
1 tablespoon vinegar or lemon juice ✦ 1 cup milk - 1 cup sour milk
10 graham crackers - 1 cup fine crumbs
1 cup whipping cream - 2 cups whipped
1 cup evaporated milk - 3 cups whipped
1 lemon - 3 to 4 tablespoons juice
1 orange - 6 to 8 tablespoons juice
1 cup uncooked rice - 3 to 4 cups cooked rice

A HANDY SPICE GUIDE
TO MAKE YOU BECOME A SEASONED SEASONER

ALLSPICE...a pea-sized fruit that grows in Mexico, Jamaica, Central and South America. Its delicate flavor resembles a blend of cloves, cinnamon and nutmeg. USES: (Whole) Pickles, meats, boiled fish, gravies. (Ground) Puddings, relishes, fruit preserves, baking.

BASIL...the dried leaves and stems of an herb grown in the United States and North Mediterranean area. Has an aromatic, leafy flavor. USES: For flavoring tomato dishes and tomato paste, turtle soup; also use in cooked peas, squash, snap beans; sprinkle chopped over lamb chops and poultry.

BAY LEAVES...the dried leaves of an evergreen grown in the eastern Mediterranean countries. Has a sweet, herbaceous floral spice note. USES: For pickling, stews, for spicing sauces and soup. Also use with a variety of meats and fish.

CARAWAY...the seed of a plant grown in the Netherlands. Flavor that combines the tastes of Anise and Dill. USES: For the cordial Kummel, baking breads; often added to sauerkraut, noodles, cheese spreads. Also adds zest to French fried potatoes, liver, canned asparagus.

CURRY POWDER...a ground blend of ginger, turmeric, fenugreek seed, as many as 16 to 20 spices. USES: For all Indian curry recipes such as lamb, chicken, and rice, eggs, vegetables, and curry puffs.

DILL...the small, dark seed of the dill plant grown in India, having a clean, aromatic taste. USES: Dill is a predominant seasoning in pickling recipes; also adds pleasing flavor to sauerkraut, potato salad, cooked macaroni, and green apple pie.

MACE...the dried covering around the nutmeg seed. Its flavor is similar to nutmeg, but with a fragrant, delicate difference. USES: (Whole) For pickling, fish, fish sauce, stewed fruit. (Ground) Delicious in baked goods, pastries and doughnuts, adds unusual flavor to chocolate desserts.

MARJORAM...an herb of the mint family, grown in France and Chile. Has a minty-sweet flavor. USES: In beverages, jellies and to flavor soups, stews, fish, sauces. Also excellent to sprinkle on lamb while roasting.

MSG (MONOSODIUM GLUTAMATE)...is a vegetable protein derivative for raising the effectiveness of natural food flavors. USES: Small amounts, adjusted to individual taste, can be added to steaks, roasts, chops, seafoods, stews, soups, chowder, chop suey and cooked vegetables.

OREGANO...the leaf of a safe bush growing in Italy, Greece and Mexico. USES: An excellent flavoring for any tomato dish, especially Pizza, chili con carne, and Italian specialties.

PAPRIKA...a mild, sweet red pepper growing in Spain, Central Europe and the United States. Slightly aromatic and prized for brilliant red color. USES: A colorful garnish for pale foods, and for seasoning Chicken Paprika, Hungarian Goulash, salad dressings.

POPPY...the seed of a flower grown in Holland. Has a rich fragrance and crunchy, nut-like flavor. USES: Excellent as a topping for breads, rolls and cookies. Also delicious in buttered noodles.

ROSEMARY...an herb (like a curved pine needle) grown in France, Spain, and Portugal, and having a sweet, fresh taste. USES: In lamb dishes, in soups, stews and to sprinkle on beef before roasting.

SAGE...the leaf of a shrub grown in Greece, Yugoslavia and Albania. Flavor is camphoraceous and minty. USES: For meat and poultry stuffing, sausages, meat loaf, hamburgers, stews and salads.

THYME...the leaves and stems of a shrub grown in France and Spain. Has a strong, distinctive flavor. USES: For poultry seasoning, in croquettes, fricassees and fish dishes. Also tasty on fresh sliced tomatoes.

TURMERIC...a root of the ginger family, grown in India, Haiti, Jamaica and Peru, having a mild, ginger-pepper flavor. USES: As a flavoring and coloring in prepared mustard and in combination with mustard as a flavoring for meats, dressings, salads.

HELPFUL HINTS

Pancakes are lighter when Club Soda is substituted for a part of the milk in the recipe. Use the remainder of the bottle to clean spots from clothes and pets, rugs.

A small dish of water in the oven will keep bread crust from getting hard.

An egg white added to a cup of cream and beaten together will almost double the volume of whipped cream.

If you keep the candles for the birthday cake in the refrigerator for a day before using, they will burn slowly and evenly.

Experienced cooks do a roast with the fat side up. The juice soaks down into the meat and keeps it basted and moist.

Do not discard worn pillow slips. Cut a small hole in the seamed end and slip it over a hanger as protection for clothes.

For black frosting for party cupcakes, add blue food coloring to your favorite chocolate frosting.

Add a little vinegar to the water when an egg cracks during boiling.

Put a layer of marshmallows in the bottom of a pumpkin pie, then add the filling. You will have a nice topping as the marshmallows will come to the top.

A pinch of salt added to very sour fruit while cooking will greatly reduce the quantity of sugar needed to sweeten them.

Whipped cream will stay firm longer if you use powdered sugar instead of granulated.

Use muffin tins to make large ice cubes for punch bowl. For even larger ice cubes, use Cool Whip containers.

BAKING POWDER: 2 T. cream of tartar, 1 T. soda, 1 T. corn starch. Mix and store in airtight container.

A leaf of lettuce dropped into the pot absorbs the grease from the top of the soup.

To rescue over-salted foods cooked in water, drop in a few slices of raw potato and boil until excess salt is absorbed

1 C. plus 2 T. dry milk, plus ¾ C. sugar and ½ C. warm water. Mix the warm water and milk well. Stir in sugar until it dissolves. This may be used whenever sweetened condensed milk is required.

Add 1 tsp. vinegar to grease when frying doughnuts. They will absorb less fat.

To make your kitchen appliances shine, use baking soda on a damp cloth to clean.

To remove coffee or tea stains from china cups, rub them with moist salt.

Ink stains on a carpet can be removed by dabbing with a little denatured alcohol mixed with white vinegar, then sponge off with warm water and detergent.

Worcestershire sauce is a good polish for brass.

Save your old toothbrushes; they're great for cleaning combs, silverware or jewelry.

You can remove crayon marks from linoleum by rubbing them with silver polish on a damp cloth.

Remove those little balls of fuzz from an old shirt collar by going over the surface with a clean electric shaver. It will not harm fabric.

For longer lasting white tennis shoes, spray heavily with starch.

A rubber band wrapped around each end of a coat hanger will keep garments from slipping off.

To prevent water spilling from ice cube trays, put a spoon in one of the compartments. Remove the spoon when the tray is safely in place.

To soften hard marshmallows, put them in the refrigerator.

Perk up soggy lettuce by adding lemon juice to a bowl of cold water and soak for about 1 hour in the refrigerator.

Eliminate fat from soup and stew by dropping ice cubes into the pot. As you stir, the fat will cling to the cubes. Discard the cubes before they melt.

Fresh eggs are rough and chalky in appearance. Old eggs are smooth and shiny.

Eggs beat up fluffier when not too cold. They should be at room temperature for best results.

When opening a can of food, try opening it at the bottom instead of the top. The contents will come out much more easily.

Red cabbage must always be cooked with something acid (lemon or vinegar) otherwise it turns a hideous color.

To keep the cut edge of cheese from drying out, spread a little butter or margarine over it.

To avoid shells cracking while boiling eggs, start them in cold water.

Revive wilted lettuce by soaking it for a half hour in cold water to which lemon juice has been added.

Ever try to climb up a greased pole? Tough, isn't it? That's why you should never grease the sides of a cake pan.

To keep bacon from curling when frying try dipping it first in cold water and then dry on a paper towel.

Dry cement, sprinkled over grease and oil spots on concrete garage floor will absorb the spots. Just sweep up the soiled dry cement.

To keep a wallet from slipping out of your pocket, wrap a heavy rubber band around it.

Keep bows and other delicate decorations in a plastic bag. Blow up with air and tie it shut. Keeps from being crushed.

Ants don't like salt. So if you're invaded by them, sprinkle salt along baseboards and in corners.

Before working in the garden, scrape your fingernails across some dry soap. The dirt will come right off with washing.

Faucet that leaks one drop per second can waste 650 gallons a year. If it's hot water, that wastes heating energy as well.

Small dents in car doors or fenders of many cars today can be repaired by using a common plumber's friend to suck them out.

You can clean clogged letters on typewriter keys by pressing a strip of adhesive tape over them, then lift it off.

A good tonic for ferns is to water them once a week with weak tea.

Use glycerin if you want to put a gloss on the leaves of your plants. It is much better than olive oil, since it does not collect dust.

To clean blades or cutter on your electric can opener, run a paper towel through the cutting process.

When a drain is clogged with grease, pour a cup of salt and a cup of baking soda in the drain followed by a kettle of boiling water. The grease will usually dissolve immediately and open the drain.

For a sparkling white sink, place paper towels across the bottom of your sink and saturate with household bleach. Let set for ½ hour or so.

To remove streaks on stainless steel sinks, rub with olive oil.

To remove stains from chrome trim on the faucets and kitchen appliances, apply baby oil with a soft cloth, then polish.

Don't throw flour on a grease fire because it could explode. The use of water on a grease fire is dangerous...Toss baking soda onto the base of the fire. First turn off source of heat.

To rid the brown grease spots from the bottom of an electric frying pan, place the pan in a large plastic bag containing a cloth saturated with ammonia. Close the bag with a rubber band, leaving the handle containing the electric element outside the bag. In a few hours, remove the pan and you will be able to wipe the spots off with ease.

To help salt flow freely with humid weather, keep a few grains of raw rice in the salt shaker.

Milk is a great food for cats...but only as a supplement. Remember it can also act as a laxative; never use it as a substiture for water.

Need a Gift?

for

• Shower • Birthday • Mother's Day •
• Anniversary • Christmas•

Turn Page For Order Form
(Order Now While Supply Lasts!)

TO ORDER COPIES OF
THE COVERED BRIDGES
COOKBOOK

Please send me _____ copies of The Covered Bridges Cookbook at $11.95 each, plus $3.75 shipping and handling. (Make checks payable to QUIXOTE PRESS.)

Name _____

Street _____

City _____ State _____ Zip Code _____

SEND ORDERS TO:

QUIXOTE PRESS
3544 Blakslee Street
Wever, IA 52658

- - - - - - - - - - - - - - - - - - - -

TO ORDER COPIES OF
THE COVERED BRIDGES
COOKBOOK

Please send me _____ copies of The Covered Bridges Cookbook at $11.95 each, plus $3.75 shipping and handling. (Make checks payable to QUIXOTE PRESS.)

Name _____

Street _____

City _____ State _____ Zip Code _____

SEND ORDERS TO:

QUIXOTE PRESS
3544 Blakslee Street
Wever, IA 52658